THE
SENCo
Handbook

Sixth Edition

This sixth edition of the best-selling *The SENCo Handbook* has been extensively updated to take account of the SEND Code of Practice (DfE/DoH 2015), recent research and implications for policy and practice in schools and for SENCos. It provides vital information, practical approaches to the SENCo role and responsibilities and perceptive analysis of issues relevant to all schools, Early Years settings and colleges. Debating and discussing how the SENCo role has changed and will change, this book will help all SENCos, head teachers and school leaders to create and implement effective whole-school policy and practice for special educational needs.

Key topics include:

- leading and managing change in SEN policy and practice
- building the capacity of class and subject teachers to meet the needs of pupils
- managing the graduated response for those with identified additional needs
- tracking and recording progress
- developing whole-school approaches to policy and practice for those with SEND
- the deployment and management of support staff
- working with children, young people and their parents
- working in partnership with a range of outside agencies and services.

Photocopiable training materials are included, as well as source lists for further reading and information. *The SENCo Handbook* is essential reading for those studying for the National Award for SEN Co-ordination, whilst more experienced SENCos will value its academic underpinning and common sense on issues that matter.

Elizabeth Cowne has been actively involved in developing and delivering SENCo training for 30 years, largely associated with the outreach courses at the Institute of Education. She was the sole author of the first five editions of the SENCo handbooks and is author of many other publications.

Carol Frankl is Managing Director of the Southover Partnership, an independent special school and support service. She is also a tutor on the National Award for SEN Co-ordination course. Carol regularly contributes to SEN publications.

Liz Gerschel has been training SENCos, teachers, teaching assistants and governors for more than 30 years. Liz helped to develop, and currently teaches, the NASENCO course for the Institute of Education at University College London. She was a Learning Difficulties Outreach Tutor at the University of Birmingham for many years and has published on SEN, governance and equalities.

THE
SENCo
HANDBOOK

Leading and Managing a Whole School Approach

SIXTH EDITION

Elizabeth Cowne
Carol Frankl
Liz Gerschel

LRC Stoke Park
GUILDFORD COLLEGE

Routledge
Taylor & Francis Group
LONDON AND NEW YORK

Sixth edition published 2015
by Routledge
2 Park Square, Milton Park, Abingdon, Oxon OX14 4RN

and by Routledge
711 Third Avenue, New York, NY 10017

Routledge is an imprint of the Taylor & Francis Group, an informa business

First edition published by David Fulton Publishers 1996
Fifth edition published by Routledge 2008

British Library Cataloguing in Publication Data
A catalogue record for this book is available from the British Library

Library of Congress Cataloging in Publication Data
Cowne, Elizabeth.
The SENCO handbook : leading and managing a whole school approach/Elizabeth Cowne, Carol Frankl, Liz Gerschel. – Sixth edition.
   pages cm
Includes bibliographical references and index.
1. Special education–Great Britain–Administration–Handbooks, manuals, etc. I. Title.
LC3986.G7C69 2015
371.9–dc23   2015002312

ISBN: 978-1-138-80894-2 (hbk)
ISBN: 978-1-138-80895-9 (pbk)
ISBN: 978-1-315-75031-6 (ebk)

Typeset in ITC Galliard Std
by Sunrise Setting Ltd, Paignton, UK

Contents

Foreword

I am delighted to write this preface to the sixth edition of *The SENCo Handbook: Leading and Managing a Whole School Approach*. I can remember the publication of the first edition and just how useful this was to the many teachers who were just embarking on their SENCo careers and needing well-informed and practical advice and guidance. *The SENCo Handbook* provided this, but it also helped SENCos to think beyond the day-to-day aspects of their role – important as these were – and to consider how they might provide the kind of whole-school strategic leadership that enabled mainstream schools to become more inclusive and effective organisations that provided high-quality educational support for all learners. The book was ahead of its time, and has stood the test of time!

The sixth edition is in many respects a new book, although key concepts and principles in the original version are still integral to its content. Liz Cowne has shared authorship in this edition with two highly skilled and experienced colleagues, Carol Frankl and Liz Gerschel, both of whom are involved in the training of SENCos and wider aspects of special educational needs and disability (SEND) focused development work with teachers, support staff, parents, children and young people. The book benefits greatly from the experience, expertise and reflective qualities of all three authors and has a vital overall coherence as well.

As we embark on a new era of special and inclusive education, working with a new statutory special educational needs and disability legislative framework introduced from September 2014 and a new SEND Code of Practice covering the 0–25 age range, demands on SENCos will increase significantly. Both the Children and Families Act 2014 and the new Code ensure that SENCos will have a high profile. This is good news, but we need to be careful in ensuring that this does not lead to overload or an over-reliance on the named SENCo. Throughout this new *SENCo Handbook* the authors share clear and practical information and advice that will help new and experienced SENCos to manage and lead the development of SEND policy, provision and practice in their schools and to do so in ways that foster collaboration and strengthen whole-school capacity to be responsive to the needs of all learners.

The SENCo Handbook is also really up to date, so SENCos can turn to it for essential information on topics ranging from implementing a graduated approach to SEND support, to writing an SEN information report, working with the Local Offer, working more closely with children, young people and their families and collaborating more effectively with health, social care and other services, as well as leading and managing change. In other words, the handbook is an excellent resource for questions such as 'where do I find out' and 'what do I do'. But it also encourages SENCos, and other professionals who will enjoy reading it, to think about their professional practice analytically and reflectively. Getting the balance between theory and practice right in a book of this kind is not easy, but the authors get it just right – I recommend the *SENCo Handbook* to any teachers who are participating in National Award for SEN Co-ordination courses across the country and to the many experienced SENCos who may be wanting to refresh their knowledge and skills in a new legislative era. It ought to be on every SENCo's bookshelf!

Christopher Robertson
Lecturer in Inclusive Education and Programme Lead for the
National Award for Special Educational Needs Coordination,
School of Education, University of Birmingham
October 2014

About the Authors

Elizabeth Cowne has been involved in SENCo training for three decades. She has worked in partnership with colleagues from Local Authorities across Greater London to develop outreach courses, running from the Institute of Education, for training and supporting SENCos in their work. She has also taught at Kingston University and the Open University on SENCo-focused courses. She wrote the first five editions of *The SENCo Handbook*, and has contributed to a range of other publications or conferences related to SENCos.

Carol Frankl has been teaching SENCos since 1999, most recently on the National Accreditation for SEN Co-ordination course. She is managing director of Southover Partnership Ltd, one of the leading providers of special needs education services in London. Carol regularly contributes to SEN publications on topics such as teaching assistant deployment and leading and managing change.

Liz Gerschel is an education consultant, trainer and writer and ex-LEA Senior Adviser. She has been training SENCos, teachers, teaching assistants and governors for over 20 years. Liz helped to develop, and currently teaches, the NASENCO course for the Institute of Education, University College London. She has published on SEN, governance and equalities.

Acknowledgements

The authors would like to thank the many colleagues from local authorities who have contributed to, or given advice on, the previous five editions of this book. We also owe a debt to the several hundreds of course members, from schools across the LAs in the Greater London Area, with whom we have worked. Their projects on aspects of whole-school policy development, carried out as part of their course work, have added in-depth knowledge of how SENCos manage change.

For this edition, we are also indebted to Chris Green (Barking & Dagenham) for her contributions, and to Paula Coates, Helen Jackson, Ingrid Redcliffe and Julie Revels for their advice and help. Thanks also to Judith Wade for updating her previous contribution on the SEND Tribunal, and to Alison Holloway and John Platts for their help in the book's production. Crown copyright material is reproduced with the permission of the controller of HMSO.

Elizabeth Cowne

How to Use this Book

The SENCo Handbook: leading and managing a whole-school approach

This book is intended to help SENCos, head teachers and governors to create and implement effective policy and practice for special educational needs in every school. This new edition has been extensively updated to take account of the SEND Code of Practice (DfE/DoH 2015), recent research, and implications for practice, schools and their SENCos.

The book provides information, practical approaches to the SENCo's role and responsibilities and perceptive analysis of issues relevant to all schools, as well as a training Activities Pack. It is an essential handbook for new SENCos studying for the National Award for SEN Co-ordination. More experienced SENCos will value its academic underpinning and common sense on issues that matter. The book can be dipped into for specific topics, as well as being read right through. Links between chapters are given in *italics* to help the reader follow themes across the book.

Chapter 1 – Decisions and Dilemmas in SEN: Legislative and Historical Perspectives

The purpose of this chapter is to outline the history of special educational needs legislation and practice, in order to examine changing perspectives and attitudes left as a legacy from the past. Selected government initiatives which impact on special educational needs policy are briefly described, especially those that led to the SEND Code of Practice (DfE/DoH 2015).

Chapter 2 – Roles and Responsibilities within Whole-School SEN Co-ordination

This chapter begins with descriptions of the roles and responsibilities in connection with whole-school SEND policy and practice. Next, aspects of the SENCo's role are discussed in more detail, including the SENCo's role in leading and managing others. These include the question of whether the SENCo is a member of the Senior Leadership Team, time management, the SEN Information Report and the

SEN budget. These themes continue in all later chapters, particularly in *Chapters 10* and *11*. *Activity 1* audits policy.

Chapter 3 – Identification, Assessment and Planning for Progress

This chapter begins by examining some theoretical aspects of identification and assessment of SEND. The graduated response of the Code of Practice (2015) (DfE/DoH 2015) is then described. The chapter ends by discussing the SENCo's role in working with colleagues. Further administrative roles are described in *Chapter 9*.

Chapter 4 – Teaching and Learning for All

Aspects of teaching and learning are discussed, and perspectives on pedagogy and differentiation considered. The implications of these perspectives are put into the framework of whole-school curriculum planning, and include high-quality teaching. *Activity 2* is a staff development exercise on lesson planning for Key Stages 1/2 and 3.

Chapter 5 – Managing Effective Support

This chapter looks at the management of effective support and is in two parts. In the first part, the nature of SEN support and the role of the Teaching Assistant (TA) is described and debated, in the light of extensive recent research on deployment and practice of TAs. The second part discusses the SENCo's role and responsibilities in managing TAs, training, monitoring additional provision and reviewing school support policy. *Activity 3* is an audit to review support policy and practice. *Activity 4* is a checklist for SENCos on managing support.

Chapter 6 – Working with Parents, Children and Young People

The chapter reflects the increased emphasis in the new SEN framework on the voice and rights of the child/young person and their parents/carers. It looks at how schools and their SENCos can work effectively with children and young people to learn about their views, feelings and wishes, and work with parents/carers to build good partnerships which improve pupil well-being and progress. The chapter describes personal skills required of the SENCo and teachers. Reference is made to 'structured conversation' with parents, taken from the Achievement for All project. Some themes in this chapter continue in *Chapter 8*.

Chapter 7 – Working with Professionals and Organisations beyond the School

The Local Offer, as defined by the Children and Families Act (2014), is explained and the various services from education, health and social care outlined, as are networks of voluntary organisations. The SENCo's role in developing relationships with outside services and agencies is discussed, particularly in the light of the new Education, Health and Care Plans. *Source List 2* provides contact details for major charities.

Chapter 8 – Working in Partnership at Transition Periods

Partnership with parents, children, young people and professionals at critical transition points in the pupils' lives is described; these are early years and entry to school, phase transfer and transition planning at 13+, including transition to further education and adult life, in line with the extensions of the SEND Code of Practice: 0–25 Years (DfE/DoH 2015).

Chapter 9 – The SENCo's Role in Leading and Managing SEND Provision

This chapter explains core aspects of the SENCo's administrative work. These include monitoring of individual planning for pupils with SEND; the maintenance of records and organisation of review procedures, associated with the SEND Code of Practice (DfE/DoH 2015); and preparation of paperwork and information to feed into reviews of the school policy or development plan, or for an Ofsted inspection. Key features of mediation services and the SEND Tribunal are also described.

Chapter 10 – The SENCo's Role in Leading and Managing Change

This chapter explains the process of change management that will support SENCos in planning and implementing changes, including those required by the SEND Code of Practice (DfE/DoH 2015). It describes managing change theoretically, politically and practically. Several models of change management are discussed, to explain ways of working with people to achieve sustainable outcomes. Action Research principles are outlined as a way of giving change management a structure.

Chapter 11 – The SENCo's Role in Developing Inclusive Practice

The chapter starts by debating issues around the concepts and practice of inclusion. It then focuses on the SENCo's responsibility for development and training of staff, and the SENCo's own training needs. Lastly, it draws together themes from earlier chapters, showing how the SENCo's skill and knowledge might help them develop inclusive practice. *Activity 5* evaluates training.

Abbreviations

ADD	Attention Deficit Disorder
ADHD	Attention Deficit Hyperactivity Disorder
AfA	Achievement for All
AfL	Assessment for Learning
ASD	Autistic Spectrum Disorder
CAF	Common Assessment Framework
CAMHS	Child and Adolescent Mental Health Service
CoP	Code of Practice
CPD	Continuing Professional Development
DCSF	Department for Children, Schools and Families
DDA	Disability Discrimination Act
DES	Department of Education and Science
DfE	Department for Education
DfEE	Department for Education and Employment
DfES	Department for Education and Skills
EAL	English as an Additional Language
ECM	Every Child Matters
EHC	Education, Health and Care
ERA	Education Reform Act
EP	Educational Psychologist
EWO	Education Welfare Officer
EYFS	Early Years Foundation Stage
FE	Further Education
HLTA	Higher Level Teaching Assistant
HMI	Her Majesty's Inspectors
IEP/GEP	Individual Education Plan/Group Education Plan
ITT	Initial Teacher Training
LA	Local Authority
LEA	Local Education Authority
LMS	Local Management of Schools
LO	Local Offer
MLD	Moderate Learning Difficulties
NASENCO	National Award for SEN Co-ordination
NASEN	National Association for Special Educational Needs
NCTL	National College for Teaching and Leadership
NUT	National Union of Teachers

Abbreviations

Ofsted	Office for Standards in Education
P levels	Performance levels
PCP	Person Centred Planning
PHSE	Personal, Health and Social Education
PMLD	Profound and Multiple Learning Difficulties
PRU	Pupil Referral Unit
PSED	Public Sector Equality Duty
RAISEonline	Reporting and Analysis for Improvement through school Self-Evaluation
SALT	Speech and Language Therapist
SA/SA+	School Action/School Action Plus
SEN	Special Educational Needs
SENCo	Special Educational Needs Co-ordinator
SEND	Special Educational Needs and Disabilities
SENIOS	Special Educational Needs in Ordinary Schools
SENSSA	Special Educational Needs Support Association
SIP	School Improvement Plan
SLCN	Speech, Language and Communication Needs
SLD	Severe Learning Difficulties
SLT	Senior Leadership Team
SMART	Specific, Measurable, Achievable, Reasonable and Time-bound
SpLD	Specific Learning Difficulties
SWOT (Analysis)	Strengths Weaknesses Opportunities Threats
TA	Teaching Assistant
TDA	Training and Development Agency for Schools
TTA	Teacher Training Agency
VAK	Visual, Auditory, Kinaesthetic

xv

CHAPTER 1

Decisions and Dilemmas in Special Educational Needs

Legislative and Historical Perspectives

This chapter looks at the history of special education in England and Wales, particularly in relation to government legislation and advisory documents. It also examines changes in attitudes towards children with a range of disabilities and discusses issues that arise from changes in policy and practice. After a quick overview of early history, we arrive at the significant 1981 Education Act, which was to change perspectives and practice, particularly in mainstream schools. In the next section the story continues, covering the next two decades, until we reach the second Code of Practice in 2001. At this point we take stock and extract themes and debates from key government documents which influenced both legislation and practice in the remaining decade or so, and which led to the third Code of Practice in 2014.

Early history

The first hundred years of compulsory schooling began in 1870 with the Elementary Education Act. In the decades which followed, pressure grew from school boards and voluntary groups to provide a separate system for educating pupils with disabilities. Children with disabilities were seen as unfit for the large classes – of 50 or more – taught by teachers with no specialist training. The usual solution was to segregate these children into special schools. Funds to run these often came from charities. By 1918, some school boards in metropolitan areas were educating the 'unfit' in special classes within normal schools. Others with disabilities were provided for by a mixture of institutions or by home visiting. The voluntary charitable societies developed professional expertise in offering vocational training, as well as care for particular groups, such as the blind and the deaf.

Special education had higher costs, so only some school boards offered provision in classes or special schools. Rural communities often kept their disabled pupils within their ordinary schools or offered no schooling at all. Universal access to education for all children with disabilities was not to come until 1970. This segregation and isolation often meant that disabled children were denied access to the normal activities and opportunities of the local school and community. In some cases, where the disabled child did attend a village school, their needs may not have been understood and they often suffered ridicule.

The 1944 Education Act

At the end of the Second World War, the 1944 Education Act was passed. The policy behind this Act was to provide statutory education at primary and secondary stages to all children, including those with disabilities. The only exceptions were those who had a severe mental handicap, for whom it took a further 26 years and new legislation to give Education Authorities the responsibility for their education. The 1944 Act stated:

> Local Educational Authorities (LEAs) should secure that provision is made for pupils who suffer from any disability of mind or body, by providing either in special schools or otherwise, special educational treatment, that is to say education by special methods for persons suffering from that disability.
>
> (See *Appendix 1a* – Categories from 1959)

The LEA was to ascertain which children needed special treatment and then decide on placement according to category. The advice used to make this decision came largely from medical officers. Later, psychologists began to be employed to test this group of children and to assist the medical officers in their decision-making. Tomlinson (1982: 29) remarked:

> the history of special education must be viewed in terms of the benefits it brought for a developing industrial society, and the normal mass education system, as well as the benefits that medical, psychological, educational personnel derived from encouraging new areas of professional expertise.

Towards the end of the period 1944–78, much had changed. A complex special education system of schools, classes and services had been built up. Teacher training in SEN specialisms had developed. Children with severe learning difficulties were at last given the right to education through the Handicapped Children Act (1970). Parents had begun, through voluntary groups, to exert pressure for change. Influences from abroad (the USA in particular) were affecting the thinking of such groups. The Warnock Committee, set up in 1974, produced a report in 1978 (DES 1978); from this grew significant legislation for special education – the 1981 Act.

The 1981 Education Act

The 1981 Act redefined the population of pupils with disabilities as those with 'special educational needs' (SEN). This Act gave clear guidelines about assessment procedures and the issuing of a Statement of Special Educational Needs, a legal document which summarises a pupil's learning difficulties and lists suitable provision. Building on the recommendations of the Warnock Report, much was said in the 1981 Act about involving parents in decision-making in relation to assessment. Schools were also given responsibilities to identify the full range of those with SEN, using the five-stage assessment procedure suggested in the Warnock Report.

The term 'special educational needs' depends on the concept of relativity of need. This is the most fundamental dilemma of special educational needs, because although the term includes children with disabilities, it also includes those whose educational progress in learning is significantly slower than that of their peer group, for whatever reason. Identifying which individuals have such needs and so require something extra or something different from what is normally provided requires a decision-making process. Provision was made across what Fish (1989) called 'dimensions of need', all of which lie on a continuum. Decision-making becomes complex when the providers of various resources have different priorities. Education, for example, may specify that health authorities should provide therapies for children with SEN, but the health authority may not see this as a priority area for their resources. This is a further dilemma which arises out of cross-professional provision: one which must be resolved on a regional or national level, and which the SEN legislation challenges and clarifies.

The 1981 Act embodied much of what had been developing over time, and could be perceived as building on 'best practice'. The 1981 Act influenced the attitudes of teachers in mainstream schools. Some began to recognise that pupils with SEN were their responsibility. Integration policies were adopted by many schools and LEAs. Training for special educational needs in ordinary schools (SENIOS) was funded through training grants from 1983 onwards (DES Circulars 3/83–86 (DES 1983, 1984, 1985)). Those responsible for special needs provision in schools were not, at this time, called special educational needs co-ordinators (SENCos). The responsibility was often taken by either a member of the senior management team, or was put in the hands of the 'remedial' teacher or team.

The 1981 Act also attached great value to multi-disciplinary assessment. The power of the medical profession and its model of deficit within the child to be remedied, which had affected special education for so long, was reduced. The focus was on educational needs, and these were to be described in educational terms and met by educational provision. 'Treatment' was not a word used in describing this provision. Guidance on assessment and Statements was given through Circular 1/83 (DES 1983). The 1981 Act required joint decision-making between health, education and social services. Parents began to have some say in their child's assessment and voluntary organisations began to lobby on behalf of different groups of children.

The Education Reform Act (1988)

The Education Reform Act (ERA) contributed to a new perspective on pupils with learning difficulties – a perspective which has radically developed since, based upon raised expectations of the learning capabilities and potential attainment of children and young people with special educational needs. The ERA (1988) stated that all children have a right to a 'broad, balanced, relevant and differentiated curriculum'. On the positive side, this meant all pupils now had an 'entitlement curriculum'. On the negative side, teachers were over-loaded by the requirement to teach the number of subjects specified and to test and assess pupils' progress in all of these subjects. Schools began to be more aware of their overall performance as judged by these tests, so pupils with special educational needs were not always seen as an asset. This Act also introduced Local Management of Schools (LMS) and from then onwards schools acquired responsibility for most aspects of funding, including the provision for children with SEN.

The 1993 Act and Code of Practice (1994): the 1996 Act

The Education Act (1993) (Part 3) replaced much of the 1981 legislation, though without significant changes. The new elements were the setting up of the SEN tribunal and the publishing of the *Code of Practice on the Identification and Assessment of Special Educational Needs*. This document had a status falling between that of a regulation, which is statutory, and a circular, which is advisory. Schools and LEAs were, and still are in later editions of the Code, required to use their best endeavours to 'have regard to' the requirements of the Code of Practice to make provision for pupils with SEN. However, then as now, certain parts were also mandatory.

The Act (1993) and Code of Practice (1994) (DfE 1994) pushed the decision-making surrounding Statement and provision further towards schools and parents, but final decisions were still made by the LEAs, who took advice from other professionals through the multi-disciplinary assessment. Parents could initiate requests for assessment and had an increasing amount of power when exercised through the SEN tribunal.

The 1996 Act replaced that of 1993, consolidating various pieces of legislation but not making major changes in relation to SEN, although it did state that schools must identify, assess and make provision for pupils with SEN. It also said that LEAs must provide maintained schools with auxiliary aids, such as laptop computers or braillers, and transport where needed.

Second SEN Code of Practice (2001a)

The Code of Practice (2001) (DfES 2001a) built on all of this experience and practice. It was differently structured to make it more accessible to readers and also included new chapters which emphasised the importance of working in partnership with parents and listening to pupils' views. This was partially due to the Children Act (1989), which, although not focused on education, was influential in changing viewpoints about children's rights and parental responsibilities. The Code of Practice (2001) included an entire chapter on pupil participation. It stated very clearly that all children and young people have rights, including the rights to be consulted, to have their views heard and to be involved in making decisions and exercising choices.

Broad categories of need were reintroduced (see *Appendix 1b*). The sections on identification and assessment were presented for three phases: early education settings; primary phases; and secondary phases. The staged assessment procedure was simplified and revised into a graduated response. The school-based stages were called *School Action* (SA) and *School Action Plus* (SA+). Interventions were to be recorded on Individual Education Plans (IEPs) for pupils at these stages and for those with Statements of SEN. The last chapter of the Code of Practice (2001) (DfES 2001a) described the working partnership between agencies.

The Special Educational Needs and Disability Act (2001b)

2001 also saw the publishing of the Act known as SENDA, which amended part 4 of the Disability Discrimination Act (1995) and introduced the obligation upon schools to publish an Accessibility Plan, showing how access to the curriculum, the environment and information would be improved, over renewable three-year periods, for pupils with learning difficulties and disabilities. The requirement to have an Accessibility Plan remains statutory and means that school planning and policies must address three distinct elements:

• improvements in access to the curriculum;
• physical improvements to increase access to education, school facilities and associated services;
• improvements in the provision of information in a range of formats for disabled pupils.

In order to ensure equality, schools are expected to make 'reasonable adjustments' to their provision so as to provide the increased access required. This duty is proactive: schools may no longer wait for pupils with disabilities and learning difficulties to arrive, but must plan ahead in the expectation that such children will be part of their regular intake. Schools must not discriminate, nor give less favourable treatment to pupils with disabilities and learning difficulties on the grounds of their disability. Excellent guidance on the duties of schools is offered in the Disability Code of Practice (DRC 2002), and the issue of what is a reasonable adjustment has been clarified by practice and by SEND tribunals and recent guidance (EHRC 2014). Much of the DDA (1995) has now been subsumed within the Equality Act (2010).

It is perhaps the definition of disability that is having the most far-reaching and inclusive effects (see *Appendix 1c*). It means that all people (children and adults) with learning difficulties are protected by the law from discrimination, as are those with disabilities and sensory impairments, those with mental health problems or those diagnosed with long-term illnesses such as cancer, even if these do not impair their learning or work.

Overall, although previous legislation had significant impact on mainstream schools in overcoming the barriers to inclusion, nevertheless barriers remain:

Although these barriers may be unintentional, that does not make their impact upon disabled people any less significant. When buildings, services and employment practices are designed in a way that fails to take into account the particular circumstances of disabled people, this excludes and disadvantages them. The same applies when budgets are set for a programme without adequately considering the additional needs of disabled people.

(DRC 2005: 1.8)

Equality Act (2010)

This Act replaced all existing equality legislation, consolidating it into a single simplified source of discrimination law. Much therefore remains from earlier Acts. Crucially, schools cannot lawfully discriminate against pupils with SEN and disability in admissions, provision of education services or exclusions on the grounds of their disability. Reasonable adjustments must be made, including provision of auxiliary aids and services to disabled pupils. Clear advice on interpreting the Act is available for schools (DfE 2014c).

Review of progress over 20 years

Over the 20-year period since the 1981 Act, SEN practice in mainstream schools developed in many significant ways. All mainstream schools (particularly primaries) expected to receive the majority of children with additional needs from their catchment areas, as this was often parents' first choice. Early Years providers had paved the way for this and helped schools prepare for the needs of the new entrants, often with input from various outside agencies from education and health services. Once in school, it was expected that access to a broad, balanced and relevant curriculum would be available to all children, suitably differentiated to meet their needs. This was further confirmed by the Inclusion Statement in the National Curriculum legislation in 1999. Parents were expected to be active and interested partners, especially in the process of reviewing their child's progress. Children's views should also have been recorded.

In practice, it could be argued that in many schools, not all of the above happened, for a number of reasons:

- Teachers and sometimes SENCos lacked training to meet the wider range of needs, so felt unable to take responsibility for all children with SEN;
- SENCos were overloaded with paperwork due to the need to write and review IEPs;
- An over-individualised needs-led approach meant that classroom teaching and learning issues were not always taken on board;
- The increased number of TAs, with little or no training, many delivering intervention programmes, resulted in poor-quality teaching;
- Perceived pressure from Ofsted and the emphasis on academic results impinged on schools' flexibility to meet children's needs, thus increasing the tensions between the inclusion and standards agendas.

Further government documents and inquiries were to look at many of these issues.

Every Child Matters: Change for Children (DfES 2004a)

Every Child Matters: Change for Children (2004a) (ECM) was the government of the time's vision for a radical reshaping of children's services and improvements in opportunities and outcomes for all children and young people, from birth to 19 years. This vision aimed to resolve some of the problems involved in multi-agency working to facilitate better information-sharing. The key objective was intervention as early as possible, to ensure the education and well-being of the whole child and prevent some children 'slipping through the net'.

The rationale of ECM was that pupil performance and well-being are interlinked, and five key areas of need for children were identified. Although ECM is not part of current parlance, the five areas have remained as reflections of pupils' well-being. Children and young people should:

• be healthy
• stay safe
• enjoy and achieve
• make a positive contribution
• achieve economic and social well-being.

Ofsted and other inspectorates have judged the contributions of all the services to improving what are called 'wider outcomes' in each of these areas, including for children with learning difficulties and disabilities.

Common Assessment Framework (CAF)

This new structure for inter-agency working was introduced in 2008. This process (using an interactive online record) helps practitioners from a range of local authority and voluntary services to work in an integrated way to obtain a complete picture of a child's additional needs at an early stage, within the context of their family's needs. Its purpose is to enable faster and better targeted referrals to specialist services and to ensure that basic information follows the child, to reduce duplication and increase safety. The CAF was mentioned positively in the Ofsted Review (2010) and continues to be used, sometimes to support statutory assessment (see *Chapter 7*).

Removing Barriers to Achievement (DfES 2004b)

The government of the time's strategy for achieving their vision to enable pupils with special needs and disabilities to succeed, wherever they live,was set out in the document 'Removing Barriers to Achievement'. The four key areas were:

• early intervention
• removing barriers to learning
• raising expectation and achievement
• delivering improvements in partnership.

This strategy was born of the Every Child Matters agenda and aimed to ensure children had a good education and regular opportunities to play within their local community. Raising expectations and achievement for SEN pupils focused on personalised learning and on the impact of interventions on pupils' learning. Staff training to improve understanding of SEN issues and provide the know-how to tackle them effectively was provided through online programmes such as the Inclusion Development Programme (see *Source List*).

A review of SEN systems

Lamb Inquiry: Special Educational Needs and Parental Confidence (DCSF 2009a)

The Lamb Inquiry focused on hearing the views of parents about their experience of the SEN system. The results were mixed and much affected by where the parents lived. While many parents shared positive views, others had experienced problems with what was seen as a confrontational system. Recommendations were made as a result of this inquiry from which an implementation plan was derived, key elements of which were:

• a focus on outcomes rather than provision itself
• strengthening of parents' voices
• local systems in tune with children's needs, and of a consistently high quality
• building accountability around children's progress.

Another outcome was the specific duty for Ofsted to report on the quality of education for those with SEND.

Ofsted 2010: The Special Educational Needs and Disability Review: 'A statement is not enough'

This review was commissioned to evaluate how well the legislative framework and arrangements served children and young people who had special educational needs or disabilities. It considered the early years, compulsory education, education from 16-19 and the contribution of social care and health services.

(Ofsted 2010)

The findings of this review were wide-reaching, looking at how those who were considered to have SEN were identified, assessed and given support for their learning, and, most importantly, whether that provision was seen to be effective in helping them to make progress. In particular, it discussed whether higher expectations and better teaching would lead to greater distinction between SEN and underachievement, and thus fewer pupils being identified as having SEN. The key recommendations made would be seen to influence policy-making and practice in the following years. Recommendations that would directly affect schools included:

• a focus on high-quality teaching and better assessment which will improve outcomes for all children;
• ensuring that schools do not identify pupils as having special educational needs when they simply need better teaching;
• ensuring that where additional support is provided, it is effective, and that there is rigorous monitoring of continued progress;
• simplifying legislation so that the system is clearer for parents, schools and other education and training providers;

- developing specialist provision and services strategically so that they are available to maintained and independent schools, Academies, free schools and colleges;
- ensuring assessment systems are consistent across services and fully accountable.

Progression guidance (DCSF 2009b)

In 2009 the government published advice on progress for children – including those with SEND – through National Curriculum levels and P levels, for the first time. Expectations for all pupils are high but realistically will not result in the same achievement levels for all; the focus is now on progress in the light of age and prior attainment for those with SEND. Schools must monitor the success of additional provision and demonstrate progress for all pupils. There is an ongoing debate regarding the space between the need to make appropriate provision for pupils with SEND that meets their developmental needs and the desire to be seen to achieve high academic levels for all.

Other reviews

Other important reviews of systems include the Bercow Review of Services for Children and Young People (0–19) with Speech, Language and Communication Needs (DCSF, 2008b), which made recommendations that have raised the focus on improved provision for pupils with SEN. The SALT Review (DCFS 2010) looked at the training provided for those wishing to teach children with SLD and PMLD.

Support and Aspiration (DfE 2011)

This Green Paper followed Ofsted's (2010) influential report and critiqued the existing SEN system, promising a vision for a radical change. The key features of the new system included:

- giving more control and choice to parents, including the choice of mainstream or special school, through publication of the local offer of services and an option of a personal budget by 2014;
- giving a voice to pupils and young people, whose views are to be sought and who are to be directly involved in decision-making about their learning;
- emphasis on learning and achievement, with promises for more specialist training for teachers and lecturers. Special schools are encouraged to share their expertise with mainstream schools;
- preparation for adulthood through planned transition within education and into adult life. Young people with SEND may continue in education to 19 and beyond if appropriate. Those with EHC plans will have access to support until age 25, including support into employment.

To trial these new systems, Pathfinder pilots were set up in sample local areas and the Green Paper also went to wider consultation. This consultation helped to refine the key elements of this reform to frame the new Code of Practice.

Pupil Premium

The Pupil Premium was introduced in 2011 to raise achievement and improve outcomes for children and young people from low-income families who are eligible for free school meals, children in council care (looked-after children) and those from families with parents in the armed forces. There is considerable overlap between children eligible for free school meals, looked-after children and those with special educational needs, and SENCos have had some input into how the funds can be best spent. Characteristic of this and other initiatives is the need to produce evidence of the effectiveness and value of the interventions and activities introduced, as increasing sums are earmarked for this.

Children and Family Act (2014)

Much of the above developing policy and practice has finally led to the Special Education and Disability Code of Practice: 0–25 years (2014) (DfE/DoH 2015). This Code relates to Section 3 in the Children and Family Act (2014) and gives statutory guidance for 'organisations who work with and support children and young people with Special Educational Needs and Disabilities'. The main additions to and themes and developments of existing practice include:

- extending guidance from 0 to 25 years to include young people's transition to adult life;
- increased participation of children, young people and their parents in decision-making at all stages of assessment, provision-making and strategic planning, and especially giving young people over the age of 16 more independence in decision-making;
- guidance for joint planning and commissioning of services between education, health and social care, including guidance for LAs in providing their Local Offer;
- new guidance on identification, assessment and support for all pupils with SEN, using a graduated response, replacing SA and SA+ from the 2001 Code;
- replacing Statements of Special Educational Need with Education, Health and Care (EHC) plans, subject to transitional arrangements lasting three years;
- responsibility of classroom and subject teachers to assess, plan, implement and review the provision and progress for pupils with SEND, whether they or TAs do the teaching. The role of the SENCo has therefore increasingly become that of co-coordinator, strategic planner and adviser to colleagues on meeting their responsibilities;
- the category of Behaviour, Emotional and Social Development has been altered and is now Social, Emotional and Mental Health Difficulties. This acknowledges the increasing prevalence of mental health needs in children and young people, and recognises that behaviour is a reflection of need rather than a need in itself.

The rest of this book will explore aspects of all these themes in more detail.

Dilemmas, debates and discussion

Parents, children and young people

Over recent decades, since the 1981 Act, there has been an ever-increasing emphasis on involving parents and listening to children and young people. The SEND Code of Practice (DfE/DoH 2015) takes this further by stating that parents must be part of decision-making, and that 'the views, feelings, and aspirations of children and young people must be taken into account' (DfE/DoH 2015: 1.1; see also *Chapter 6*). Clearly, involving parents and listening to children and young people should be a whole-school issue for all parents and children, not just those with SEND. Many schools already do this well. For other schools, making this work in practice may be more challenging and will require cultural changes. If successful, the practice of consulting children and parents, and acting on their views, will be embedded throughout the organisation of the school day and year.

Language of disability

Ways of describing disability have changed over the past century, and certain terms are no longer acceptable. 'Labelling' children with any disability name, however – or indeed with the term SEN itself – has some dangers: individual differences are ignored or self-esteem may be reduced by making the children 'different' in the eyes of others. Some parents value having a label, because it helps explain problems their child is having and may provide access to resources and support groups; other parents, however, may not wish for their child to be described as disabled. Teachers too may welcome a label, for similar reasons, but seeking one can encourage a 'within-child' approach (as will be explored in *Chapter 3*) instead of recognising the influence of the school environment. There may be a tension between identification and assessment processes in wishing to find such a label and the discrimination or 'otherness' this produces. Teachers also need to consider how much they reinforce 'otherness' through lower expectations or in-class groupings, as well as in the language used to describe needs. For example, it is preferable to refer to children with SEN than to talk of SEN children. This theme continues in *Chapter 11*.

Developing the SENCo role

Between 1983 and 1994 the role of the SENCo became fully established, and a description of the role was written into the first Code of Practice (1994) (DfE 1994). In 1998 the Teacher Training Agency (TTA) published the *National Standards for Special Educational Needs Co-ordinators*, which set out the core purposes of the role of the SENCo and the key outcomes of SEN co-ordination. These standards enhanced the role of the SENCo, giving it a higher profile. They were also used as guidelines for SENCo training courses and in fact formed the basis of the National Award for SEN Co-ordination when it was introduced in 2009. The SENCo is no longer focused solely on classroom teaching and learning – nor are learning support teachers – but has instead become a strategic part of whole-school planning and management, leading, developing, co-ordinating and monitoring provision made by colleagues. The SENCo does not act alone on behalf of all pupils with SEND, but rather through the shared responsibility of the whole school: truly a SEN-Co and not a 'SEN-Do' (Gerschel, 2010). The knowledge and skills needed by the SENCo to fulfil this role, and what it entails in terms of policy, process and practice, will be the focus of this handbook's remaining chapters.

CHAPTER 2

Roles and Responsibilities within Whole-School SEN Co-ordination

This chapter introduces the theme of roles and responsibilities in mainstream schools, Academies and free schools for pupils with special educational needs and disabilities, as defined in the SEND Code of Practice (DfE/DoH 2015) and related legislation. This includes the roles and responsibilities of the governors and headteacher or proprietors, as well as those of the SENCo and other staff, as all teachers have responsibility for those pupils in their classes with special educational needs. Parents, pupils and ancillary staff also have contributions to make. The overall responsibilities lie with those who are legally responsible for the school – the governing body, the headteacher and the Senior Leadership Team (SLT) – and those who carry out the strategic planning for the school's development. Co-ordination of the day-to-day policy and practice for SEN is the responsibility of the SENCo, but it is important to recognise all of the above as part of a whole-school approach to SEN co-ordination.

Effective schools manage special educational needs by being clear about their priorities when allocating and monitoring roles and responsibilities. Effective school policies also depend on good communication systems between all those holding these responsibilities. The school moves forward in its development by integrating special needs policies into the school improvement plan as a whole. Effective schools remain so by being reflective organisations which manage change. This requires a mixture of flexibility and consistency. The challenge of SEN is that of constant change and the necessity to adapt not only to the needs of the pupils, but also to new ways of looking at pupil progress.

Governing bodies' duties

Whatever arrangements are made in a particular school, statutory duties remain with the governing bodies of maintained schools, Academies and free schools. These duties are variously laid out in the Education Act (1996) and the Children and Families Act: SEND Regulations (2014). It is good practice, although not statutory, to have a Governor Committee to ensure that statutory requirements for SEN are met and to consider, and report on, the school's general policy and approach to meeting children's SEN.

The SEND Regulations (2014) require governing bodies and proprietors to include specified information in an SEN Information Report on the school's website, which **must** be updated annually. This school report includes much of the information that would previously have been in the school's SEN policy, but there are notable additions, such as:

- including more detailed information on the school's policies for identification, assessment, planning teaching approaches and reviewing provision for pupils with SEN (whether or not the pupil has an EHC Plan);
- information on the expertise and training of staff with regard to SEN, and about how external advice and support will be secured;
- arrangements for consulting and involving parents and children and young people, including how they are involved in policy review:
- the school's arrangements for supporting children and young people when transferring between phases in education or in preparation for adulthood and independent living;
- guidance regarding how to access the local authority's Local Offer.

See *Appendix 2a* for the full Schedule 1 Regulations 51 (2014).

Equality duties

Governors have additional responsibilities in law, relating to their role as:

- employers of people with disabilities;
- providers of education to their disabled pupils;
- providers of a service to other disabled users of the school, including parents and the community.

The Equality Act (2010) is a single, consolidated law which identifies nine protected characteristics, of which disability is one. It has introduced a Public Sector Equality Duty (PSED), which governors must follow. They must have due regard to the need to:

- eliminate discrimination and other conduct that is prohibited by the Act;
- advance equality of opportunity between people who share a protected characteristic and people who do not share it;
- foster good relations across all characteristics – between people who share a protected characteristic and people who do not share it.

These requirements protect pupils, staff and others with disabilities in the school community. Some, but not all, pupils with disabilities have special educational needs. The disability provisions in the Equality Act mainly replicate those in the former Disability Discrimination Act (DDA), but there are some differences that governors and SENCos should note (see *Appendix 2b*) – in particular, that the failure to make reasonable adjustments for pupils with disabilities can no longer be justified and that schools may now have to provide auxiliary aids and services. Schools must still have an Accessibility Plan, as is necessary under the DDA and replicated in the Equality Act 2010. Accessibility plans, which are anticipatory, must be aimed at:

• increasing the extent to which disabled pupils can participate in the curriculum;
• improving the physical environment of schools to enable disabled pupils to take better advantage of education, benefits, facilities and services provided;
• improving the availability of accessible information to disabled pupils.

These equality-related provisions are the responsibility of governors and may very well be part of the strategic planning, leadership and management role of the SENCo.

The role of the Special Educational Needs Co-ordinator

The role of the SENCo and the concept of a whole-school policy for special educational needs have both developed over the decades since 1983. All government-maintained schools, academies and free schools must now accept that they have responsibilities for special needs and that someone has to be named as their SENCo, even though this may mean the roles they hold are doubled or even trebled. Independent schools are also more aware of these responsibilities, and many have appointed SENCos and developed SEN policies.

In 1998 the Teacher Training Agency published National Standards for the teaching profession. The National Standards for SENCos listed key areas of SEN co-ordination:

• strategic direction and development of SEN provision in the school;
• teaching and learning;
• leading and managing staff;
• efficient and effective development of staff and resources.

These are still relevant to the SENCo role and training.

SENCo regulations

The House of Commons Education Skills Select Committee report on SEN (2006) recommended that SENCos should in all cases be qualified teachers and in senior management positions in the school. The committee also recommended that SENCos should be given ongoing training to keep their knowledge up to date, as well as sufficient non-teaching time in relation to the number of children with SEN in their school. Some of these recommendations became statutory when the first SENCo Regulations came into force in 2008, followed by mandatory training in 2009. This was further enforced by the SEND Code of Practice (DfE/DoH 2015), which says:

> A newly appointed SENCo must be a qualified teacher and, where they have not previously been the SENCo at that or any other relevant school

15

for a total period of more than twelve months, they must achieve a National Award in Special Educational Needs Co-ordination within three years of appointment.

(DfE/DoH 2015: 6.85)

(See *Appendix 2c* for list of key SENCo responsibilities.)

National Award for SEN Co-ordination

This mandatory award must be accredited by universities, and individual courses may be chosen by local authorities or schools. Courses are designed to support professional development and help improve practice. Key components of the new SEN system should be covered, as well as the learning outcomes of the National Award set out by the National College for Teaching and Leadership (see *Appendix 2d*).

The SEND Code of Practice (DfE/DoH 2015) adds that a National Award must be from a postgraduate course accredited by a recognised higher education provider. When appointing staff or arranging for them to study for a National Award, schools should satisfy themselves that the chosen course will meet these outcomes and equip the SENCo to fulfil the duties outlined in this Code. Any selected course should be at least equivalent to 60 credits at postgraduate study level.

Early Years SENCos

Since the publication of the 2001 Code of Practice, Early Years settings must have an appointed SENCo and have access to the Area SENCo. Maintained nursery schools must ensure that their SENCo is a qualified teacher who has the prescribed NASENCo qualification. Ofsted-registered Early Years providers have a duty under the statutory framework for the Early Years Foundation Stage (EYFS) (DfE 2014b) to have and implement a policy and procedures to promote equality of opportunity for children in their care, including support for children with SEN or disabilities.

The SEND Code of Practice (DfE/DoH 2015) specifies that the role of the EY SENCo is to:

• ensure all practitioners in the setting understand their responsibilities for children with SEN and the setting's approach to identifying and meeting SEN;
• advise and support colleagues;
• ensure parents are closely involved throughout and that their insights inform action taken by the setting;
• liaise with professionals or agencies beyond the setting.

The SENCo as a member of the senior leadership team

Despite continuing government recommendations that membership of the school's SLT is advisable for SENCos, this has not become statutory. The reasons for this may be sound. What becomes clear from research (Mackenzie 2007; Tissot 2013) is that the SENCo role cannot be generalised and that diversity is the norm. This could be due to a number of factors, such as:

• the phase, size and geographical setting of the school;
• the amount of available time to carry out the role – some SENCos are part-time; many are full-time class teachers;
• the expertise and experience of the SENCo (particularly management skills);
• the priorities and ethos of the school, headteacher and proprietors.

A study by Oldham and Radford (2011) examined the views of a sample of secondary SENCos on leadership. Although many are not members of the SLT, most aspired to be. These SENCos felt that the influence of senior staff was important, especially that of the headteacher. It was also noted that there is a trend in secondary schools for distributed leadership, where different aspects of the school are the responsibility of a number of leaders. The SENCo may well be seen as leader of the support team, but this could reduce their universal role in relation to SEN policy and practice across the school.

Where the SENCo is not part of the leadership team it is essential that there is good communication and collaboration between the SENCo and that team, so that information is shared and the SENCo feels supported.

Layton (2005) reminds us that one of the core features of the TTA Standards (1998) was the assumption that the SENCo would be an agent for whole-school SEN policy. Research by Layton and Robertson found that the SENCos in their sample did not believe that key people and agencies saw them in that leadership role, although they were expected to manage SEN matters. Reference to Fullan (2003) and Layton (2005) introduces the term 'moral purpose', 'which for SEN leadership ensures motivation to effect changes in the lives and aspirations of all pupils'; SENCos in their sample 'found the greatest barrier to achieving their moral purpose as SENCo was identified as not being a member of the SLT' (Layton 2005: 59).

This was reinforced later by Tissot (2013), who advised that the SENCo needs to have a role as a strong leader in a school to advocate for students with disabilities over the pressure of other priorities. Although the SEND Code of Practice (DfE/DoH 2015) recommends that 'The SENCo has an important role to play with the headteacher and governing body, in determining the strategic development of SEN policy and provision in the school. They will be most effective in that role if they are part of the school leadership team' (DfE/DoH 2015: 6.87), it is the governing body who must determine the SENCo's relationship to the leadership and management of the school, and therefore whether the SENCo is a member of the SLT. Where the SENCo is not a member of the SLT it is expected that a 'champion' will ensure that SEN issues are raised and addressed.

All teachers

There is a strong emphasis in the SEND Code of Practice (DfE/DoH 2015) on all teachers being responsible for those with SEN in their classes. This is certainly a whole-school issue and the SENCo's status may well need to be reviewed, along with other aspects of SEN policy.

> High quality teaching that is differentiated and personalised will meet the individual needs of the majority of children and young people. Schools and colleges must use their best endeavours to ensure that such provision is made for those who need it. Special educational provision is under-pinned by high quality teaching and is compromised by anything less.
>
> (DfE/DoH 2015: 1.24)

The SENCo will have a role in strengthening teachers' knowledge and skills, which may include 'reviewing, and where necessary, improving teachers' understanding of strategies to identify and support the most vulnerable pupils and their knowledge of SEN most frequently encountered' (DfE/DoH 2015: 6.37).

Time as a resource

SENCos cannot carry out their responsibilities without adequate time outside the classroom. Time is an issue under constant discussion, both in the relevant research and among SENCos. There are two separate elements to this:

- first, the time allocated to the role by the school management;
- second, the question of how this allocated time is to be used and tasks prioritised.

The National Union of Teachers' SEN survey (NUT 2004) asked many questions about SENCo non-contact time. As in previous surveys, the picture is complex, depending on school size, population and other roles held by the SENCo. The amount of time allocated ranged from a full timetable to 2–4 hours a week. The reasons given for insufficient non-contact time were ranked as follows: first, school priorities lay elsewhere; second, lack of finance; third, other commitments (teaching and non-teaching).

Research continues to show that it is still the case that a large proportion of SENCos in primary schools are also full-time class teachers (Szwed 2007; Tissot 2013) or combine this role with many other responsibilities – often that of deputy head. The Code (2015: 6.91) (DfE/DoH 2015) states that 'The school should ensure that the SENCo has sufficient time and resources to carry out these functions'. This is because so many of these duties require liaising with a variety of people – parents and carers, colleagues and pupils, professionals from out-of-school services. The new emphasis in the Code of Practice (2015) (DfE/DoH 2015) on pupil voice and parent participation will require additional SENCo time to develop.

The Code also says that schools should provide the SENCo with 'sufficient administrative support and time away from teaching to enable them to fulfil their responsibilities in a similar way to other

	Urgent		Not Urgent
1	Activities: • Crisis • Pressing problems • Deadline-driven projects	2	Activities: • Prevention, PC activities • Relationship building • Recognising new opportunities • Planning, recreation
3	Activities: • Interruptions • Some calls • Some mail • Some reports • Some meetings • Proximate • Pressing matters • Popular activities	4	Activities: • Trivia • Busy work • Some mail • Some phone calls • Time wasters • Pleasant activities

Figure 2.1 Time Management Matrix.

Source: Adapted from Covey (1989).

important strategic roles within a school' (DfE/DoH 2015: 6.91). It is not cost-effective to deploy the expensive SENCo resource when a trained clerical assistant can do much of the filing, appointment-making and record-keeping. Figure 2.1 offers an analysis of SENCo activities and time.

Being off-timetable does not mean never entering classrooms – indeed, observing, monitoring and evaluating provision and team or lead teaching may be essential, but this is not possible if the SENCo is a full-time class teacher, or has only half a day per week for the role.

Workload

More than a decade of research shows that SENCo overload is a recurrent theme. This is unlikely to change with the new Code's requirements. This means time management is essential for a SENCo. As Frankl (2008) advises, this should begin with taking stock and considering goals and visions. For example, Rosen-Webb's (2011) research suggested that SENCos' core values focus on interest in how learners learn, so making them key players in teaching and learning development in their school. It is all too easy to let the daily routine and the need to deal with urgent matters take over, while overlooking what is important.

Building a team approach to whole-school SEN co-ordination means that SENCos must lead and share duties using all available resources and skills, keeping a balance between administrative and bureaucratic activities and working creatively with pupils, colleagues, parents and outside agencies.

The SEN budget

Over the past decade it has become increasingly important for SEN-Cos to understand their school's SEN budget and contribute to strategic decisions in relation to its use. The NUT (2004) survey mentioned above found that schools lacked the necessary expertise in issues related to SEN funding. The survey found that greater clarity was required so that headteachers and SENCos were aware of the exact amount provided and how to use it appropriately. The Code of Practice states: 'The SENCo, Head teacher or proprietor should establish a clear picture of the total resources available, including pupil premium' (DfE/DoH 2015: 6.97).

A notional SEN budget is allocated centrally to mainstream schools, who are expected to meet the needs of pupils with high-incidence (low-cost) needs. From this notional SEN budget, the school will be able to contribute the first £6,000 of additional costs for high-needs pupils. Funding above this level will be agreed with the LA and paid from their High Needs block (Schools Funding Reform: Arrangements 2013–14, DfE 2012c). Schools have some freedom as to how money is allocated, but should be able to account for how this funding is spent and what difference it has made. LAs have a statutory duty to monitor and evaluate the effectiveness of schools' SEN provision and expenditure.

The SENCo's salary should be costed to the school's salary budget and not be paid from SEN funding, although there are some exceptions. A high percentage of SEN pupils also draw Pupil Premium funding, and SENCos need to be aware of how this double funding is impacting on outcomes for pupils. A costed provision map using average costs for TAs is a useful way to demonstrate how various funding streams are used.

Experience and research shows that many SENCos do not feel empowered to become involved in policy and funding decisions. They may not have access to information or may not feel they can ask for it. In these cases the strategic SEN co-ordination is in the hands of the head and governors, so it will be important to ensure that the head teacher and governing body have up-to-date information about the numbers of pupils receiving SEN support and their needs. Provision mapping can be an efficient way of demonstrating the range of additional and different types of support given and what they cost. Costing will usually be annual, although termly updates may be necessary where the school population is transient.

Data analysis

Schools are becoming increasingly data-rich. The challenge for SEN-Cos and class teachers is to know which data they need, when they need it and how to analyse the data they have. Data on its own has little meaning or value but, once intelligent questions are asked, it can provide some useful information. This information can then be used to formulate analyses that help empower SENCos in their day-to-day work. Data is useful at many levels, from the whole-school or macro level to the individual pupil or micro level. It is always useful to begin with the big-picture data.

National annual SEN data collection is carried out within schools' January censuses. However, changes as a result of the SEND Code of Practice (DfE/DoH 2015) meant that from 2015 the January data collection would be slightly different, with schools required to submit the following data:

• the total number of pupils receiving SEN support;
• the number of pupils with SEN without a Statement or EHC plan;
• the number of pupils with a Statement or EHC plan;
• a breakdown by area of SEN for all pupils receiving SEN support.

The data submitted every January forms part of the national SEN data published annually every summer, which can be found at https:// www.gov.uk/government/collections/statistics-special-educational-needs-sen.

Data must be accurate to be useful. The national SEN dataset determines the national funding allocation for SEN, so the SENCo must have oversight of the January SEN data before it is submitted. Data on pupils' needs will inform the school of the provision it needs to have in place and empower the SENCo's decision-making. Pupil performance data from subject leaders (in secondary schools) or class teachers (in primary schools) will help build a picture of individual learning strengths, weaknesses and levels of independence.

The point of gathering all this information is to identify clearly the next steps in learning for pupils. The SLT and SENCos must together establish:

• what information most helps teachers track children's progress;
• how best to collect and analyse information;
• how to use the analysis to evaluate and adjust the teaching and lesson design to meet individual needs (see *Appendix 2e*).

Leading, managing and training support staff

An aspect of the SENCo role which has developed significantly since the Code of Practice (2001) (DfES 2001a) is leading, managing and training of support staff. Over the past two decades there has been a large increase in the number of additional staff working in schools (see *Chapter 5*). The National Standards for SENCos stated that SENCos should take an active part in leading and managing staff. Specifically, they should:

> Advise, contribute to and, where appropriate, co-ordinate the professional development of staff to increase their effectiveness in responding to pupils with SEN, and provide support and training to trainee and newly qualified teachers in relation to the standards for the award of Qualified Teacher Status, Career Entry Profiles and standards for induction.
> (National Standards for Special Educational Needs Co-ordinators, TTA 1998:13)

The SENCo regulations (2014) state that SENCo responsibilities include selecting, supervising and training learning support assistants who work with pupils who have special educational needs and contributing to in-service training for teachers at the school to assist them in carrying out their duties (see *Chapter 5*).

Developing and maintaining a whole-school approach

Reviewing the SEN policy

The SEN policy should begin with a mission statement reflecting the school's beliefs and values around SEND. The rest of the policy should explain how this is to be put into practice and how parents, pupils and teachers can be partners in the process. This will mean considering and redefining the existing roles and responsibilities across the school, starting with class and subject teachers and how they carry out their role of identifying, assessing and planning for those with SEN in their classes. Next there should be an evaluation of the SENCo's role in supporting teachers and managing all the various aspects of their responsibilities as listed in the SENCo regulations (see *Appendix 2c*). The SLT might ask if the SENCo is part of their team, or should be. Mackenzie (2007) suggested that the effectiveness of the SENCo's role might be evaluated here, while recognising that a lot of the SENCo's work is not easily measurable. However, evaluation is now statutory for the Governing Body (see *Appendix 2c*).

Developing these roles and co-ordinating the whole-school approach will evolve over time. Schools will be at different stages of development in this process; therefore, it is important to evaluate what each school has achieved. The next step is to review what is in place and see what must be added. Another step may be to check staff understanding and knowledge of the school's existing SEN policy and practice and evaluate what each believes:

a) *should* be in the policy
b) is *actually* the case at present (see *Activity 1 – Whole-School Policy*).

Policy means intended action, but it is based on a value system which may mean changing the attitudes of some or all staff, and such change takes time. Each year, the policy must be evaluated against the success criteria of the previous year (see Figure 2.2).

Monitoring and evaluation

It is the statutory duty of governors to publish the School Information Report in a way that is accessible for parents (as explained earlier in this chapter). This information is likely to form a major part of their policy document. SENCos are likely to play an important role in collating this information and keeping it up to date – which is not a task to be carried out by the SENCo alone. If the policy is to be meaningful and reflect practice, all members of the school community should have opportunities to express their views and contribute to policy development. SEN policy should not exist in isolation, so part of the evaluation will be to see how it fits with other school policies and the school improvement plan. If policy is to remain active and dynamic, it must be seen as a process of development. This requires maximum involvement of the headteacher and senior management team, representation from the curriculum and pastoral systems and the co-ordination of practice by the SENCo. If effective, the whole-school policy is likely to enhance the teaching, learning and well-being of *all* pupils

Figure 2.2 Policy Review Cycle.

and to link with other existing policies, such as those for equality or behaviour. There should also be a strong relationship with the assessment policy, teaching and learning policies and curriculum planning.

SENCos who are members of the SLT should be involved in this process and make sure that SEN is not sidelined, and that practice reflects policy. This could give SENCos an opportunity to include SEN issues and to select aspects of provision for improvement, as part of the ongoing cycle of evaluation of the SEN policy and practice. Whatever self-evaluation systems schools use, the process is vital to help strategic planning and efficient use of resources. Developments and changes in the school's policy and practice must be made known to the governing body by the head teacher or SENCo, and the governors must include this in their information report.

Reviewing targets

If targets in the previous year have been set with clearly intended outcomes and success criteria, then it will be easy to see what has been achieved. It is therefore important, when choosing targets for SEN policy as part of the School's Improvement Plan (SIP), to:

a) make these small and precise enough to be achieved;
b) review what is in place and what must be added, such as criteria or indicators so that success can be recorded or lack of success investigated;
c) allocate roles and responsibilities for the implementation of the target;
d) set a time-scale for implementation;

e) identify how progress towards achieving the targets will be monitored;

f) evaluate how successful the school was in reaching this target.

Inclusive school systems

Schools can be defined as open systems, which include parents and communities as part of the system. Some schools can include more of their community within the school than others. This depends on the knowledge, competence and confidence of staff; the trust that parents and the community have in the school; and effective policies of support and communication. It also depends on the value system of the governors and senior management team, and how these pervade the whole school. It is said that a school that is effective for pupils with SEN is usually effective for all pupils. Such a school will support staff and parents' needs as well as those of the pupils. It will run efficiently and standards and expectations will be high. Such a school is likely to have a more inclusive policy for pupils with problems or differences (this theme continues in *Chapters 6* and *11*).

CHAPTER 3

Identification, Assessment and Planning for Progress

Identification of those with Special Educational Needs (SEN)

The Children and Families Act (2014) defines children as having special educational needs if they have a learning difficulty or disability which calls for special educational provision to be made for them, including:

- having significantly greater difficulty in learning than the majority of others of the same age;
- having a disability that hinders them making use of educational facilities provided for others of the same age.

The SEND Code of Practice (DfE/DoH 2015) clarifies this to say the only children who should be considered to have special educational needs are those for whom it was necessary to make provision that is additional to or different from that normally available to children of the same age. So, the starting point of all work in SEN is identification of those whose needs will be met through the graduated approach as given in the new Code. Identification will be made through regular assessment of pupil progress by class and subject teachers. Less than expected progress could be defined as that which:

- is significantly slower than that of their peers starting from the same baseline;
- fails to match or better the child's own previous rate of progress;
- fails to close the attainment gap between the child and their peers;
- widens the attainment gap;
- does not respond as expected to the curriculum on offer.

Once a pupil with SEN has been identified, the first response should be high-quality differentiated teaching targeted at areas of weakness. Information gathering and assessment take place and this contributes to a planned intervention aimed at reducing barriers to learning or to accessing the curriculum. SENCos have a major role in advising and supporting class teachers in planning suitable strategies. Part of this process will be to collect data about an individual child using existing records, including assessments carried out as part of usual school practice or for national data. At this point parents or carers must also be informed, and their views and those of the child or young person noted.

The SEN Regulations (2014; see *Appendix 2a*) list the information that must be made available in relation to SEN provision in the school. This includes policies regarding identification of and assessment and provision for pupils with SEND, and arrangements for monitoring and reviewing the effectiveness of provision. Those with Statements or Education Health and Care Plans (EHC) for whom the school is responsible must have annual reviews.

The SEND Code of Practice (DfE/DoH 2015) requires all class and subject teachers to raise any concerns with their SENCo that they may have regarding high-quality teaching not meeting a child's needs. In discussion with the SENCo and parents, decisions will be made about additional provision, an agreed plan of action drawn up and expected outcomes agreed. While all children have individual needs, these are not necessarily all related to learning difficulties or disabilities as defined by the various Acts. There are some children for whom the definition of SEN may not be appropriate, as discussed below.

English as an Additional Language (EAL)

Children for whom English is not their first language may still be developing their bilingual ability. At the early stages of this process, access to the curriculum as delivered is difficult. These children do not necessarily have learning difficulties; indeed, they may be very efficient learners. If these learners are at the early stages of learning English, they should *not* be considered as having SEN.

The SEND Code of Practice (DfE/DoH 2015: 6.24) says that schools should look carefully at all aspects of a child's performance and learning, to establish whether lack of learning is due to limitations in their command of English, SEN, or both. Speaking to the child's parents is essential in order to understand their perception of the child's progress. It will be important to find out how long the child has been learning English and how the child functions using their home language. It should be possible to arrange assessment in the child's own language through local services. Pupils should be encouraged to use their own language as well as English (see *Appendix 3*).

Able pupils

Able or gifted pupils need a differentiated curriculum. Their needs should be identified and met by providing opportunities for extension and problem-solving, and delivery of the curriculum in a way which challenges them. Schools should have a separate policy for able and gifted pupils, and curriculum planning which takes account of such pupils: they do *not*, however, have learning difficulties, and should *not* be seen as having SEN. However, there may be gifted children who have other problems or disabilities, or 'dual exceptionality'. In these cases there will be other reasons to consider their needs for monitoring and further assessment. This is particularly the case when performance changes and is not what was previously expected. Montgomery reminds us that:

> gifted pupils with special needs exist and are more widely found than perhaps expected . . . . the most obvious sign of difficulty is the special need; the other, the giftedness, is regarded as a bonus, but they can cancel each other out.
>
> (Montgomery 2003: 5)

Underachievement

Early identification of special needs is an important aspect of ensuring the best provision is made for all children, but can in itself be problematic. There is sometimes a tension between what are thought to be special educational needs and underachievement. The legal definition says that those with SEN will require provision that is 'additional to and different from' other children of the same age. However, there are factors which could contribute to different rates of progress, including summer-born children, those living with high levels of deprivation and, indeed, children reaching developmental milestones at different times. These factors can make the distinction between SEN and underachievement blurred – a point commented on in the 2010 Ofsted review. Whole-school debate to clarify the difference between SEN and underachievement is a very worthwhile activity.

Model for inclusive practice

Initially in school it is generally the class or subject teacher who will raise a concern about a child, although in some cases it may be the parent or carer. Teachers will need to have a good grasp of the '3 Waves' model of teaching (see Figure 3.1), where Wave 1 is High-Quality Teaching (HQT) delivered through a well-differentiated curriculum that meets the needs of all pupils. Wave 1 teaching is premised on the Inclusion Statement in the National Curriculum (DfE 2014a) which expects teachers to set suitable challenges for all children, respond to pupils' needs and overcome barriers to learning. Wave 2 is for children

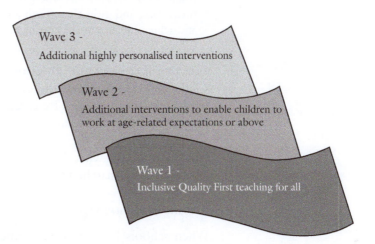

Figure 3.1 Model for Inclusive Practice.

who are underachieving, who are close to age-related expectations and should catch up with booster classes. Wave 3 is SEN Support, which could be an intervention or additional support in class.

Where SEN support is provided, either from within the school's own resources or from outside providers of, for example, speech and language therapy, occupational therapy or physiotherapy, it is important for the school to monitor the effectiveness of provision and its impact on pupil outcomes. It is an expectation of the SEND Code of Practice (DfE/DoH 2015) that class and subject teachers can evaluate how any gains made are generalised to all learning, by setting realistic outcomes before additional provision is made.

Assessment

Our present school population is probably the most tested in the world. The government links the assessment process with their agenda of standard-raising; however, a direct link between testing and progress is not clear. Testing pupils does not in itself raise standards; it is changes in the teaching and learning process that will do this. Most tests are summative in nature – they are useful for administrative purposes, to collect and compare data, and result in teachers being kept under continual pressure to produce 'results'. The type of assessment that has been proven to make a difference in enhancing performance is formative in nature. Formative assessment gives feedback to the learner and tells the teacher how to teach the next step. The Educational Endowment Fund research has shown constructive feedback to be an effective way to improve pupil performance, but, as Black and Wiliam (1998: 7) argue, 'the political commitment to external testing of teachers and schools in order to promote competition through league tables has a central priority, whilst the commitment to formative assessment is probably a marginal feature'. Formative assessment is a continuous process of monitoring each pupil's performance, noting strengths and weaknesses and planning future lessons in the light of them:

> Whilst [formative assessment] can help all pupils, it gives particularly good results with low achievers where it concentrates on specific problems with their work, and gives them both a clear understanding of what is wrong and achievable targets for putting it right.
>
> (Black and Wiliam 1998: 9)

Learning intentions for all lessons need to be as clear as possible. Clarke (2001) states that the clarity of these are essential and must be shared with the pupils. Research has shown that children are more motivated if they know and understand the learning intentions, but, as Clarke highlights, there is a difference between what teachers want children to *do* and what they want them to *learn*. Learning intentions also need to be matched to children's abilities.

Personalised learning

When schools have good assessment systems for all pupils, those with additional or different needs are more easily identified. More detailed assessment may then be necessary to find out what barriers to learning apply, and to develop effective strategies to overcome these. A successful and relevant reflection of the ideas in this chapter is the Assessment for Learning (AfL) strategy (DCSF 2008c), which introduced the concept of personalised learning to increase pupil participation and motivation and to raise standards. It is not about individualising learning for each pupil, though this may be necessary for certain pupils some of the time. The aim is to bring the locus of control nearer the student, which will affect the intrinsic motivation of the pupil and therefore their will to learn. This reaffirms the case for formative assessment techniques. The five components of personalised learning are:

- assessment for learning that feeds into lesson planning and teaching strategies;
- a wide range of teaching techniques to promote a broad range of learning strategies;
- curriculum entitlement and choice;
- organisation of school (e.g. workforce remodelling);
- partnerships beyond the school.

Discussion of these matters continues in *Chapter 4*.

Special Needs assessment models

Special needs assessment has traditionally used two models and purposes: the medical model and the curriculum model (sometimes called dynamic assessment).

The medical model

The medical model uses a diagnostic approach that produces a label for a disability or difficulty. It was originally used by the medical profession: specific physical or sensory impairments were identified using clinical judgements, sometimes backed by standardised tests. The language of the medical model still uses terms such as diagnosis, remediation and treatment. Certain types of diagnostic testing are helpful in analysing difficulties when used by competent professionals.

Category labels may also be used to assign pupils to a specific type of special school or provision. For certain physical and sensory disabilities, or for those with communication and interaction difficulties, this 'medical model' may be of use in helping to decide types of provision, including therapies. However, when defining needs in the other two categories – cognitive and learning needs and social, mental health and emotional development needs – the medical model is less appropriate.

The curriculum model

The curriculum model makes fewer assumptions about the difficulty being 'within child' than the medical model does. This model recognises that the teaching and learning process is interactive and that teaching strategies and learning styles have an important part to play in overcoming barriers. Curriculum-based assessment began to be frequently used after the publication of the 1981 Act and eventually became the platform for the Individual Education Plan (IEP) of the first Code of Practice (1994) (DfE 1994). Based on behaviourist theories of learning, it often used task analysis to break down complex activities into easily learnt steps. This meant the child was assessed on what he/she could do, at the same time as being helped to achieve target objectives. Praise was given as each small step was achieved, thus building on success. Teachers were encouraged to assess children on aspects of learning which were causing concern and to set precise targets to be achieved, stating what type of support strategies would be used and specific time limits. This approach, sometimes called 'precision teaching', is now only used in specific situations; however, some of the basic principles of this model are embedded in the 'Assess, Plan, Do, Review' cycle of the new graduated response.

The strength of using a curriculum-based approach to assessment is an important one: it tells us what a child can do, and this can then be used to plan the next steps in teaching. If this is combined with monitoring the effects of mediated learning – that is, supporting the child so that they can understand how to learn – then we have a dynamic assessment process. One of the best known examples of this type of assessment was Feuerstein's (1980) Learning Potential Assessment Device (LPAD). Feuerstein believed the task of assessment was to explore the potential for modification by mediated learning; thus, in his model, assessment and teaching are intertwined.

Identifying categories of need

Early Years identification

Parents' early observations are crucial, as are regular health visitor checks, in picking up concerns regarding possible SEND. Specialists may visit homes to provide support and training for parents. Some children may also require support at home. Information for such provision will be available from the Local Offer (see *Chapter 7*). From the age of three, many children attend early educational settings. The Early Years Foundation Stage framework (DfE 2014b) sets out the statutory requirements for these, which include identification and support for children with SEND. Each setting should have an Early Years SENCo, or access to the Area SENCo, who will help to develop targeted plans for the child.

At the end of the EYF Stage (the term before the child turns five), a profile is built up of every child, providing a well-rounded picture of the child's knowledge, understanding and abilities. This profile will assess each area of development, and the information will be available to Reception/Year 1 teachers. The profile must be shared with the parents and must, on request, be given to the Local Authority. There are four broad areas of need identified in the SEND Code of Practice (DfE/DoH 2015); however, children or young people may fall into more than one of these groups (see *Appendix 1b*).

Broad categories of need

The DfE collects information about the numbers of pupils in the country by SEN category through the Annual School Census, and this information is used to help planning, to study trends and to monitor outcomes of initiatives and different interventions. It is available annually through Statistical First Release (SFR) at www.gov.uk/government/collections/statistics-special-educational-needs-sen. The SENCo may also be responsible for listing those needs according to the categories given in the Code (see *Appendix 1b*). Consideration should also be given to disability definitions. A proportion of disabled children and young people also have a SEN. Where this is the case, access arrangements and other adjustments should be considered as part of SEN planning and review.

Communication and interaction

In this category are children with speech and language difficulties, including those who have difficulties with receptive and expressive language and those on the autistic spectrum, including Asperger's. Many of this group will have been identified in pre-school years and may already have a Statement or, in the future, an EHC plan. For those in this group, schools work closely with professionals from the health services, and in particular speech and language therapists (SALT), both to aid identification and to help in planning.

Cognition and learning

These are children whose rate of learning is slower than expected, including those with profound and multiple learning difficulties, severe learning difficulties, moderate learning difficulties and specific learning difficulties such as dyslexia and dyspraxia.

Children and young people with severe learning difficulties (SLD) and profound and multiple learning difficulties (PMLD) will have been identified before entering school, and many will be educated in settings where high levels of adult support are required for both personal care and educational needs. Moderate Learning Difficulties (MLD) is an imprecise category definition, as many children in this group will have other disabilities, such as communication difficulties. They are likely to be working below the level of their age group. Use of P levels (in National Curriculum assessment) will be appropriate for all these groups.

A child or young person with a Specific Learning Difficulty (SpLD) may have difficulty with one or more aspects of learning. This includes a range of conditions such as dyslexia (difficulties with reading and spelling), dyscalculia (difficulties with maths), dyspraxia (difficulties with co-ordination) and dysgraphia (difficulties with writing). Many children may be slow to read and write, for a number of reasons. This does not mean that they should be labelled as dyslexic – their difficulties should be assessed and met by the school's normal provision, including good teaching that takes individual learning styles into account, noting which strategies are effective. Only when all of this does not result in progress may further specific assessment be needed.

Children with social, emotional and mental health difficulties

Children and young people experience a range of social and emotional difficulties that manifest themselves in different ways, including challenging behaviour, being withdrawn or self-harming. These behaviours may reflect underlying mental health difficulties such as anxiety or depression. Other children may have disorders such as Attention Deficit Disorder (ADD), Attention Deficit Hyperactivity Disorder (ADHD) or attachment disorder. The SEND Code of Practice (DfE/DoH 2015) sees behaviour as a pointer toward another underlying need and not as a need in itself, except where it has been diagnosed by health professionals – as may be the case in, for example, ADD and ADHD. Many pupils' learning difficulties are caused by their emotional state or by their inability to learn appropriate behaviour. Pupils may be continually off-task, sometimes disrupting others, sometimes only themselves. Such pupils often have low self-esteem and poor learning strategies.

Observation and time to talk with the child in a relaxed atmosphere may pave the way to curriculum-based assessment. Good record-keeping for pupils with social, emotional and mental health difficulties will note information about:

• the pupil's learning style;
• relationships with peers and adults;
• relevant information from parents about the pupil in the home context;
• the pupil's attitudes to learning (can they risk failure?);
• observation about the pupil's strengths which can be used to build better self-esteem;
• how this pupil can be helped to function more effectively within the class.

Assessment of these children may also include diagnostic tests carried out by either those from the medical or psychological professions or teachers who have expertise in the particular area. SENCos should become familiar with the local services from which such help in assessment can be obtained (see *Chapter 7*). Careful observation, discussion with parents and records of previous development will be of great use in such assessments. Useful diagnostic tools include the Boxall Profile and the Strengths and Difficulties Questionnaire (see *Source List*).

Sensory and/or physical, including medical conditions

This is a wide-ranging set of needs including physical and sensory impairments. Minor adaptations to the curriculum and environment often suffice and may be required as reasonable adjustments under the Equality Act (2010). The majority of children in this category are likely to have been diagnosed prior to starting school, sometimes shortly after birth. However, in the case of lower levels of impairment (e.g. hearing) it may only be in the school environment that the disability emerges. Careful observation by teachers is essential in discovering whether there is such lower level impairment. Where there is a change in behaviour it is wise to check for sensory or physical difficulties which, if missed, may lead to greater problems.

The graduated approach to SEN support

The SEND Code of Practice (DfE/DoH 2015) explains the 'Assess, Plan, Do and Review' process as a four-part cycle for making provision. This is called the *graduated approach*. It states that the assessment process is threefold, focusing on:

• a clear analysis of the pupil's needs;
• information from the school's assessment and experience of the pupil;
• parents' and pupils' views.

The assessment will include desirable outcomes for the child and should be reviewed regularly (DfE/DoH 2015).

Understanding the learning context

Assessment, for those with significant difficulties, must provide enough detail to help plan carefully so that progress can be made. This will mean understanding of each disability or difficulty, and the barriers to learning that must be overcome. The total learning context for the pupil must be taken into account. This includes noting relationships with parents and teachers and features related to home and school environments. It is very important to include notes on the child's own view of their learning and the problem they think they may have. Questions to ask of assessment are:

• How does this relate to real classroom activities?
• How does this relate to long-term realistic goals?
• Is what is being tested relevant to the learner themselves and will it enhance or damage their self-esteem?
• Can this type of assessment be carried out within the time and with the staff resources available?
• Are cross-curricular skills being assessed?
• Can the pupil access the curriculum on offer?

Planning for those with Additional Needs

Most children with SEN will be planned for through high-quality teaching. Class and subject teachers can, using formative assessment, differentiate success criteria to monitor pupil progress effectively for all but those with the most complex needs. By recording progress against the learning outcome, summarising learning on teachers' planning sheets on a termly basis becomes manageable. Parents and children, where appropriate, will be included in this process. Individual planning, in the form of Person Centred Planning (PCP), need only be created for those with access needs where they require something that is additional to or different from the rest of the class in order to access the learning taking place. PCPs will be written for pupils with EHC plans. Friswell (2014) recognises that IEPs may still be used in some primary schools but advises finding new ways of working and recording progress, suggesting, for example, the development of student passports, which aim to engage the student in discussion.

Outcomes and reviewing

All planning for SEN support and for those with EHC plans will focus on outcomes (DfE/DoH 2015: 9:64, 6:40). Outcomes describe what changes are expected as a result of provision, and should be SMART. A good question to ask is 'What changes will occur as a result of the provision?' Where individual planning does take place through a PCP or behaviour plan, a review cycle should be agreed involving the teacher, parent, pupil and, where appropriate, the SENCo. Class and subject teachers remain responsible for working with SEN children on a daily basis even where children receive one-to-one support or are withdrawn from the classroom. Assessment of interventions' impact is within the remit of the class teacher, supported by the SENCo, who may undertake further assessment where necessary and provide advice on additional strategies and interventions.

Where the existing teaching and additional strategies result in reasonable progress, in line with expectations using the graduated approach, then additional provision can be ceased. If not, further assessment may be required to advise on additional or different strategies for support, or possibly referral for an Education, Health and Social Care assessment (EHC) (see *Chapter 9* for more detailed information about EHC plans).

The SENCo's role in supporting colleagues

The needs of teachers have to be met if they, in turn, are to meet the needs of children, especially those children who are more difficult to teach. Galloway (1985) defined children with special needs as those children that caused teachers stress, either because they could not learn and make progress as expected or because they could not conform to the behavioural norms expected by the teacher. Teacher stress has been exacerbated by pressures caused by league tables and performance management. Successful teachers are often seen as those whose pupils achieve or exceed national expectations in attainment. Those with learning and behavioural difficulties can impact negatively on teacher self-image.

When a whole-school approach is working, there are already many positive features in place, such as colleagues who have gained competence in meeting individual needs, a good culture of working collaboratively with parents and effective recording systems. Colleagues need someone to share concerns, so listening skills will apply here, as will problem-solving strategies. Often colleagues only need to be reassured that they are doing the right thing. The opportunity to describe their problem and express their concerns and anxieties may be sufficient to produce the feeling of being supported. It may be wise to follow this up with observation of the child or group in question. Fuller assessment may be part of the solution, or an interview with pupil and parents will often be indicated.

It is not the SENCo's role to know all answers to all questions. What they can do is facilitate the problem-solving abilities of their colleagues and help them find solutions which they feel will work. These solutions may require the SENCo to work collaboratively with the class or child or to request precise advice from services outside the school on strategies or resources. The ability to enter into productive dialogue with colleagues is the skill the SENCo will need to develop most. It is, of course, more likely that the SENCo will also have knowledge of a particular strategy or resource to help a particular child if they have experience of a variety of SEN themselves. With greater inclusion, SENCos are required to be aware of a wide range and depth of needs (see *Chapter 11* and *Source List*).

This chapter has been concerned with the responsibilities of teachers for pupils with SEND whose needs are met through careful identification, assessment and planning, then by reviewing progress. This assessment and recording process is *every* teacher's responsibility, but the SENCo must keep comprehensive records and ensure the review process is carried out thoroughly. In order for this to be possible, overall planning of time for reviews, organisation of paperwork and clear definitions of roles and responsibilities need to be part of the whole-school policy for SEN and must link to the school's assessment policy.

CHAPTER 4

Teaching and Learning for All

The previous chapter concentrated on identifying, assessing and planning for those with additional/different needs. This chapter concentrates on understanding various theoretical aspects of teaching and learning and how these might apply to the development of high-quality teaching, including the challenge of meeting most needs within classroom teaching. The problem for class and subject teachers is that for much of their day children are not taught as individuals, but in social groupings of up to 30 or more. The teaching and learning process is therefore interactive. Within-child features play their part, but so do classroom organisation and resourcing, modes of curriculum delivery and teacher management style. Some educators, such as Bruner and Vygotsky, think that learning is best conceptualised as a social process, rather than an individual one. Gipps(1992: 3) explains that 'the social constructivist model of learning assumes that knowledge is built up by the child in the form of connected schemata; the child is seen as an agent of his or her own learning activity constructing knowledge'.

One of Vygotsky's key concepts was that of the 'zone of proximal development' (Vygotsky 1978). This describes the gap between what the child can do alone and what they can do with someone who has more knowledge or skill. Gipps further explains that

> Vygotsky's model suggests that not all tasks should be perfectly matched to the child's current level of development, indeed some tasks should require a shift to the next 'zone of development' (ZPD). But what is crucial to this idea, is that interaction with another person is essential, whether this person is a teacher or peer, to help move this moving-on process.
> (Gipps 1992: 4)

This explanation of how children learn is useful in the context of providing support to teachers. The ZPD varies between children and relies on a variety of factors, including their attitude to learning and the quality of the relationship between learner and teacher. Pupils do better when they share an active part in their learning and take responsibility for their learning at an appropriate level. SENCos can coach teachers on how to involve pupils in their learning experiences and how to build positive trust: a prerequisite for learning to take place.

This suggests that a key role for the teacher is to build a rich learning community in the classroom. The classroom is also part of the wider community of the school and the district. It must, however, be remembered that influences beyond the school, both locally and nationally, affect the focus of curriculum delivery and its assessment.

The National Curriculum and differentiation

Teaching was powerfully defined in DfES (2003) as: building on what learners already know; making learning vivid and real; making learning an enjoyable and challenging experience; enriching the learning experience; and promoting assessment for learning. When the National Curriculum was first introduced in 1988, it was to be broad, balanced, relevant and differentiated, and develop knowledge skills and understandings. After decades of changes in implementation and content, these principles still largely apply. The 2014 curriculum introduces the intention to prepare children and young people for independent adult life. Teaching methods and content are prescriptive and it is important that the flexibility to meet individual needs is retained.

If the curriculum is too narrow or teaching methods too singular, this can result in lowering self-esteem and learning capacity, and can stifle creativity and motivation. Overemphasis on testing can reduce both the breadth and the balance of the overall curriculum offered. The content of the curriculum must be seen to be relevant to the learners and must take account of their developmental age, culture and interests, and the curriculum should be differentiated to give access for all learners. The National Curriculum Inclusion Statement of 2014 has two principles:

• setting suitable learning challenges;
• responding to pupils' diverse learning needs and overcoming barriers to learning and assessment for individuals and groups of pupils.

Historically, differentiation meant different outcomes for different groups, more time to complete work and different levels of support for pupils, but not always with sufficiently high expectations for SEN pupils. Effective differentiation is based on assessment: not a generalised version, but rather one based on analysis of the learner's present skills, competences and knowledge in relation to the requirements assumed for the teaching of a special topic or aspect of the curriculum. The learning intention for each topic should be clearly expressed, along with assumed prerequisite knowledge and skills.

Assessment information should show the possible gaps in these prerequisites for individuals with SEN. These may be different in each topic. Differentiation is then the process of either filling in these gaps or finding other ways to provide access to the learning required (see *Activity 2*). For example, could the way in which information is given to the learner, or recorded by them, use technology? There cannot be only one way to teach a skill or topic. As Wedell (2014) says, teachers should be guided by what works for individual children.

Government circulars and documents continually remind teachers that a flexible approach to differentiation is essential to cover the wide range of ability and experience and to take account of personalised learning. Teaching and learning have few mentions in the Code, but the importance of high-quality teaching is emphasised (DfE/DoH 2015: 6.37), as discussed in *Chapter 3*.

This will require SENCos to be able to provide advice and support about effective differentiation techniques. Effective differentiation is tied up with good assessment and, where learning outcomes are planned, based on pupils' previous learning and success. Each pupil's journey toward achievement of the learning intention may be different, depending on their attitude and learning style (this is discussed further later in this chapter). Teachers can be supported by SENCos in setting suitable learning outcomes and negotiating success criteria, alongside other measures to overcome barriers to learning. These may include additional support – which has to be carefully thought out so that SEN pupils are not working with teaching assistants for a large part of their week. The Code states that where the interventions involve group or one-to-one teaching away from the main class or subject teacher, that teacher should still retain responsibility for the pupil (DfE/DoH 2015: 6.52).

SENCos will also want to discuss with teachers how learning from interventions carried out outside the classroom can be monitored across all areas of learning. It is important to ensure that pupils do not spend too much time away from the classroom, as this will impact on their progress across all curriculum areas (see *Chapter 5* for fuller discussion).

Wragg had a useful method of conceptualising the curriculum. He started with three propositions: that education must incorporate a vision of the future; that there are escalating demands on citizens; and that children's learning must be inspired by several influences. These took him to his final proposition: that 'it is essential to see the curriculum as much more than a collection of subjects and syllabuses' (Wragg 1997: 2). This led him to propose a curriculum with different dimensions, of which the subject dimension is the first, cross-curricular issues the second and teaching and learning styles the third. This model has much to offer as a way of including the developmental and whole-child aspects so necessary for special needs work. Wragg reminded his readers that pupils are partners in the process of change and improvement, as they need to know about how to think and learn so they can become autonomous learners with the ability to work and live in harmonious groups.

Therefore, it must be remembered that the curriculum covers all aspects of learning carried out in school, not just the National Curriculum. A broad view of education would show that it is about learning how to learn and to adapt to changing circumstances. This means that SENCos should support and encourage staff to make lessons more inclusive by changing teaching styles to increase pupil participation in the process of learning.

Personalised learning

Personalised Learning is defined as high-quality teaching that is responsive to the different ways in which students achieve their best.

One principle is that every child's needs should be assessed and their talents developed through diverse teaching strategies. The initiative was researched by Sebba *et al.* (2007), who found that schools saw learning approaches as endorsing current activities or providing a means to further develop existing ones. An example of this was the reorganisation of TAs and learning mentors to provide more flexible support. Best practice features included pupils taking more responsibility for their learning and pupil 'voice' being embedded across all five AfL components. Part of the research with schools concluded that 'the centrality of pupil voice came through the work and led schools to construct their improvement plans around pupil concerns'. Many aspects of this whole-school approach had been piloted by the Assessment for Learning (AfL) initiative (DCSF 2008a) and these principles can be seen as those embedded in what is currently termed 'High Quality Teaching' (HQT) (see also *Chapter 3*).

Other commentaries on the initiative focus on the need to see it as a matter of motivation and the need to respond to differences in learning styles and pace. It is also about pupil autonomy, over both what they learn and how it is learned. The aim is to move the locus of control nearer the student and to keep an open dialogue with the learner. There can be a conflict between the two government agendas of standards and personalised learning. Wedell (2005) discusses the necessity for schools to achieve flexibility as recognition of pupil diversity. This means overcoming the rigidity of systems arising from the government's Standards Agenda, and in particular the overemphasis on testing.

Learning styles

A learning style is a method particular to an individual that is presumed to be of most benefit to them. It is therefore suggested that teachers find out about the learning styles of their students and adapt their teaching to give opportunities for each to have some choice in how they learn. One model emphasises the sensory modalities of incoming stimuli: visual, auditory, kinaesthetic – often known as 'VAK'. If material is presented in a mixed modality, the learner can then choose their favourite route.This is sometimes called multi-sensory teaching, and will affect the choice of resources and activities. Too rigid a labelling of students' styles should however be avoided because, although it is assumed that learners have a preferential style, most people use a mixed modality.

'Learning to learn is not a single entity or skill, but a family of learning practices that change ones capacity to learn' (Hargreaves *et al.* 2005: 7). Most involve the use of 'metacognition', which is the capacity to monitor, evaluate, control and change how one thinks and learns. 'Most of what teachers do in helping students to learn consists of strengthening their metacognitive capacity' (Hargreaves *et al.* 2005: 8). Although there are many popular 'packages' of material, teachers should adopt a more critical approach and look for reliable evidence-based research on impact and value.

MacGilchrist and Buttress (2005) describe a large research project in which a group of primary schools in Redbridge transformed

'Learning orientation' *Concern for improving one's competence*	'Performance orientation' *Concern for proving one's competence*
• Belief that effort leads to success • Belief in one's ability to improve and learn • Preference for challenging tasks • Derives satisfaction from personal success at difficult tasks • Uses self-instruction when engaged in task	• Belief that ability leads to success • Concern to be judged as able, concern to perform • Satisfaction from doing better than others • Emphasis on normative standards, competition and public evaluation • Helplessness: evaluate self negatively when task is difficult

Figure 4.1 Orientation Table.

Source: Watkins *et al.* (2001).

learning and teaching. This book is well worth reading in its entirety, but has some key messages that relate to the theme of this chapter. A key element of the Redbridge project was to change the culture from a performance-related one-to-one with a learning orientation (see Figure 4.1).

Another element was to teach the children the 'language of learning' and help them all reflect on the process of learning. This was achieved by listening to children's views about their learning and adopting a positive approach based on the mantra 'we can if' – meaning that success is always possible when the conditions and techniques are right. Rigorous self-evaluation in the networked learning community was crucial. This project demonstrated how successful a 'whole-school approach' (or, in this case, a four-school approach) could be. It depended on good leadership from the headteacher, but also distributed leadership across the school.

Some alternative ways of thinking about pedagogy

The second half of this chapter looks at ways of conceptualising pupils' learning within a differentiated curriculum. Approaches are discussed which may help focus on learning styles or experiences, rather than attainment levels, within a set content-based curriculum. The approaches discussed cover three ways of thinking about learning: a) behavioural; b) cognitive, in particular thinking skills programmes; and c) affective, considering the emotional needs of the learner.

The influence of behavioural science on SEN curriculum and pedagogy

Since the 1980s, special needs curriculum planning and pedagogy have been strongly influenced by behavioural theories. Based largely on applied behavioural analysis, these are a development of Skinner's operant-conditioning theory of learning. Skinner (1974) believed that by manipulating the environment, you could change an organism's behaviour: you began by deciding on the goal to be reached, and then shaped the behaviour by a system of reinforcement of successive approximations toward that goal. The reinforcement was food in work with pigeons or rats, but could be praise when working with people! Skinner argued strongly that his 'science of behaviour' could include a world view on how the environment influenced man's behaviour, and indeed his culture.

During the 1980s educational psychologists, in particular, promoted an applied behavioural approach to the analysis of learning difficulties and their remediation. Sometimes called precision teaching, this approach had been successful in special schools for those with learning difficulties. Teachers wrote precise, small-step behavioural targets, set success criteria and stated under what conditions the learning would take place (i.e. with how much support). This approach, when well executed, did break down barriers to learning for some children, who gained both confidence and mastery of certain aspects of the curriculum, which helped change attitudes to other aspects of learning. However, it was very labour-intensive, requiring individual or very small-group teaching and preparation. Moreover, not all types of learning lend themselves to such a prescriptive, teacher-led approach which takes so little account of individual learning styles or preferences. The point here is that the outcomes are chosen and predetermined by the teacher, and the child is 'shaped' toward these outcomes by the process of rewarding successive steps. This task analysis approach became firmly embedded in the IEP approach in the second Code of Practice (2001) (DfES 2001b).

Wedell (1978) encouraged teachers to negotiate with learners about objectives and to observe pupils' preferred learning styles. The fear of a mechanistic and technical approach to education remains. So how can the experience of using the behavioural approach continue to be useful to those planning the differentiated curriculum for SEN?

- objectives thinking has led to a clearer conceptualisation of individual priorities and clearer definition of needs;
- baseline assessment has been a useful starting point on which to build specific programmes to overcome barriers to learning;
- goal and target-setting, if carried out in partnership with the pupil and teacher, can increase self-worth and the child's responsibility for monitoring achievement. Evidence can be collected through observation to prove achievement;
- planning small steps to achieve success has proved worthwhile with the developmentally young or where the task is skill-based;
- individual priorities and goals can feed forward to inform both curriculum planning and differentiation and help teachers think about appropriate strategies to help pupils meet their targets.

This behavioural model of learning has strongly influenced the ways in which teachers have planned target-setting for those with SEN and, now, all pupils. One shortcoming is that by concentrating only on what can be observed, little account is taken of inner processes of thinking and feeling. Not only does this feel sterile; it also discounts huge areas of human activity and culture. The behavioural model is also very 'teacher-led', giving only limited autonomy to the pupil. There is therefore an argument for considering alternative approaches to teaching and learning; for example, a model which enhances the cognitive thinking process through planned teacher meditation.

Cognitive development and thinking skills programmes

Piaget's theory of cognitive development states that a child goes through stages: first concrete operational and then, in adolescence, formal operational thinking (Inhelder and Piaget 1958). The debate about Piaget's stages and ages lies outside the scope of the present discussion: suffice it to say that Piaget and others who extended ideas on cognitive development (Bruner 1968; Donaldson 1978) had significant effects on the pedagogy of the primary 'process' curriculum. However, it is the move into formal operational thinking which is most important in secondary education, and which may cause problems for those with learning difficulties.

Cognitive interventions based on formal operational thinking

Formal operational thinking emerges during the secondary school years. It is mediated through environmental and social interaction, but is not tied to any particular subject area. The most significant attempt to intervene and change the learning potential of young people of this age group was made by Feuerstein in the 1950s. Building on a mixture of psychometrics and the theories of Piaget and Vygotsky, Feuerstein evolved a solution to the sociological problem of new immigrants arriving in Israel. These young people were not able to take places in the traditional education system and were initially labelled as backward. Feuerstein, a clinical psychologist, challenged both the traditional trust in IQ tests and the view that intelligence was a once-and-for-all endowment. Feuerstein *et al.* (1980) said that the thinking skills we need in order to learn effectively, which are normally absorbed by children as they develop in their family and culture, can, if absent, be instrumentally remedied. Feuerstein developed a theory of mediated learning experiences and a programme of structured exercises known as Instrumental Enrichment (IE), which were free of subject content.

His work opened up a whole new field of cognitive education which spread beyond Israel to many countries, including England, and was evaluated by a Schools Council publication (Weller and Craft 1983). One project published the materials known as Somerset Thinking Skills (Blagg *et al.* 1988) that help pupils to synthesise information, analyse data and appreciate their own strategies of thinking. In England, cognitive intervention programmes could not remain free of subject content due to pressures of time and the National Curriculum and the need for teachers, pupils and the public to see results measured in improved and increased attainment in subject assessments.

Multiple intelligences

Gardner (1993) laid out a theory of multiple intelligences critiquing IQ tests, which he felt did not capture the full range of human intelligences. Gardner proposed eight dimensions of intelligence – Visual, Spatial, Musical, Verbal, Logical/Mathematical, Interpersonal, Intra-personal, Kinaesthetic and Naturalist. Multiple Intelligences (MI) theories influenced educational applications, some in ways which Gardner himself did not intend – teachers should be cautious and critical of over-simplified application of such theories. However, MI has proved popular and has helped teachers become more aware of individual differences in learning. This is particularly important for children with additional needs or disabilities.

Lessons to be learned from cognitive interventions

What, then, are the lessons that can be learned from cognitive interventions and cognitive analysis of pedagogy? The answers may include that:

- underachievement may be due to a lack of suitable strategies for thinking;
- pupils *can* be taught thinking skills if the *how* of learning (meta-cognitive)is addressed as well as the *what*;
- thinking skills can be taught through curriculum subjects, where the use of analogy can help concept development;
- when pupils are taught thinking processes, they gain control of their own learning and this increases motivation and self-esteem.

To do all of the above, teachers will need to learn how to:

- identify the stage of cognitive development reached by a pupil or group;
- examine the demands of the curriculum content and materials on offer and adapt these to individual needs;
- mediate learning through group discussions and by direct teaching of strategies to improve thinking processes;
- teach pupils to reflect on and vocalise their own thinking processes.

Affective perspectives

Emotional states are an important part of the curriculum, for many reasons. Wragg argues that emotional development could be considered as a subject on the curriculum or a cross-curricular issue, and that it certainly is something that pupils and teachers must understand: 'In positive form, emotions offer a stimulation and enhancement to pupils' learning, in negative form they can be a killer of it' (Wragg 1997: 81).

Goleman (1996) described emotional intelligence as self-awareness, impulse control, persistence, zeal and motivation. Ways of developing this, or *emotional literacy*, have influenced the approaches taken to children and young people's emotional and social development, including Personal, Health and Social Education (PHSE), nurture groups and Circle Time. Children with SEN often have low self-esteem and are particularly vulnerable to bullying. They need help to explore their own feelings and those of others, to enjoy their school experience and achieve their potential. They must trust those around them and feel safe to take risks in learning. It is essential that schools work with the peer group to help them understand those with disabilities. Many aspects of the curriculum can also feed children's emotional growth by helping them to understand emotions in themselves and others, explore the nature of relationships and make sense of how people overcome obstacles.

Opportunities can be given to explore affective responses to particular themes. The world of story, poetry, dance and drama, art and music – all have a therapeutic role to play, as well as being part of the cultural entitlement of all pupils. Sometimes artistic subjects are seen as having lower prestige than subjects which represent instrumental spheres of knowledge, such as science, but it is important that areas of understanding which have a personal characteristic are valued to the same degree. It is often through creative activities that pupils who were otherwise unremarkable begin to shine and achieve. Once this happens, the growth in self-confidence can be harnessed for their less favourite subjects. The other virtue of creative subjects or teaching methods is that they allow open-ended outcomes which are not predetermined, and pupils' individual achievements can be accepted. Differentiation by outcome is the norm. These aspects of the curriculum can feed the child, enrich language and ideas and encourage creative and problem-solving responses. They come nearer to the Early Years experiences of play, especially when taught by enthusiastic teachers.

Hanko (1995) suggests that accounts of experiences of concern to pupils can be introduced, and through discussion children can speak of their own experiences but also explore in general terms what is reflected in the literature provided. She suggests that this will also help teachers understand causes of behavioural problems. Approaches such as Circle Time (www.circle-time.org.uk) and Circles of Friends are useful techniques here.

O'Brien and Guiney (2001) assert that pupils usually have a range of 'self-esteems' and that an understanding of this complexity will be necessary to teachers in the management of emotional differentiation. The authors write about 'self-esteems' to make the concept less negative and more holistic. Learners often have different self-esteems in relation to different activities; for example, a pupil may have low self-esteem in relation to literacy, but high self-esteem in a sporting activity. This view of self-esteems recognises that individuals' feelings will also vary over time, as well as in different contexts. The authors suggest a mapping technique may prove useful to develop emotional differentiation.

Building self-esteem means having high expectations for those with disabilities or SEN. This requires the child or young person to believe in themselves and their ability to achieve. Dweck (2012) explains how mindset can affect this. The learner has to recognise that sometimes failure, or finding something difficult, may be part of the learning experience, but that failure can be overcome with a growth mindset rather than a fixed one. Giving SEN pupils too little challenge will not help their learning.

All of the above takes place within the social context of the classroom. Managing this environment so that it produces a positive influence on pupils' thinking, feeling and learning is *the* key skill for the teacher. The environment must be flexible enough to foster learning and support autonomy, and structured enough to give security to pupils and to set boundaries. Effective classrooms set within effective schools will support all pupils, but especially those with SEN. Fundamental to all of this is a whole-school culture and ethos which values individuals and allows everyone – teachers and pupils alike – to contribute to the learning process, being in fact a learning school. It must be recognised that emotional and social factors affect all learning, and connections between feelings, reasoning and learning should be developed as a whole-school policy.

The SENCo's role in developing an inclusive curriculum

Increasing participation

Cowne (2003) argues that the challenge to teachers is to increase participation in learning for all pupils. This will require knowledge and understanding of each pupil's existing skills, such as being able to listen, follow instructions, problem-solve and understand concepts. When young children enter the school system they are usually eager to learn. However, they may experience a sense of failure or frustration if they can't carry out a task or don't understand exactly what is required, or because they are not given enough time and no longer feel in control of their learning. Fear of failure can 'creep in' and a continued sense of failure then leads to a reduction in motivation, resulting in either passive learners or those who choose to 'act up' as a diversion for learning. It is important to ensure that lack of motivation does not arise from unrecognised disabilities or unmet needs. There may be reasons that are triggered by emotional insecurity or differences in home/ school cultures. Perceptions from a variety of sources, including those of the child, their family and other professionals, are needed to build up a picture of the learning situation for these individuals. Increasing participation is also about having a positive learning environment, with choice available to pupils in terms of tasks, resources, approaches and pace. It is also necessary to recognise what participation can encompass for some pupils. Perhaps an individual cannot fully complete all tasks but may be able to show enjoyment of classroom experiences. It is essential to record these small steps in engagement.

Developing positive learning environments

For any curriculum to be delivered effectively, a positive learning environment is essential. This in turn requires pupils to fit in with normal classroom routines and rules and to respect the rights of others. Certain pupils with learning or social/emotional needs present a challenge to teachers. It is outside the scope of this section to explore class management in depth; the important point to remember is that curriculum aims include the promotion of spiritual, moral, social and cultural development of all children. It follows that helping children learn how to work in a harmonious way, so that everyone is respected and valued, is part of the entitlement curriculum.

Develop a learning institution which is responsive to feedback

This means making full use of records and assessment information to plan schemes of work and lessons. In many cases this will require detailed knowledge of individual pupils and their progress, which may come from learning support staff and their observations and from listening to pupil views. At a strategic level this requires liaison time to be built into the timetable so that effective planning can take place concerning delivery of the curriculum. The DRC Code (2002) makes it clear that schools have a duty to ensure equality of access to the curriculum, as this is a right of all pupils. For the SENCo to be effective in educational rather than administrative terms is therefore a challenge. But it could be argued that it is only when those with detailed knowledge of individual differences and learning styles meet with those who plan and deliver lessons that changes to teaching and learning will occur.

Involve the parents and pupils in the curricular planning process

One of the three strands in the AfL project to improve the success of children and young people with SEND is to increase effective engagement of parents in their child's education, using a technique called 'structured conversation' (this is further explained in *Chapter 6*).

Parents are very aware that schools should remember individual needs when planning curriculum delivery. Parents of pupils with complex needs often have different priorities for their child. These concern personal, social and life skills. Parents can also problem-solve and have particular roles to play as they see their child from a different perspective than that of the teacher. Parents can remind teachers to think in a cross-curricular way so that the child is not totally overwhelmed or confused by different approaches to topics. The curriculum and its delivery may produce stress for some pupils, which could be unhealthy. For example, too much or unsuitable homework may cause pupils and parents to spend too long on this task. Some pupils react adversely to change and need preparation, which parents can provide if they are involved early enough. Parents know, for example, how long ordinary tasks such as eating and dressing can take for some children with complex disabilities. All of these types of information can be used when planning for individuals, but they may also have more general implications for school policies (see Wedell 2006).

In recent years it has been increasingly recognised that children and young people have important contributions to make to decisions about their own learning. This is strongly reinforced throughout the SEND Code of Practice (DfE/DoH 2015). Most schools ensure that pupils are consulted and their views are heard. Some schools have adopted the principles of person-centred reviews in their annual reviews.

Develop a team approach to curricular planning

Support is often the method of differentiation most chosen for special educational needs work. Support can be conceptualised as support for the pupil, but also as curriculum support with the class teacher. Best practice involves support personnel and teachers working as a team. The team can be extended to include visiting specialists, such as peripatetic teachers and therapists for those with more complex needs. The role of this team is to be as creative as possible in integrating the special requirements of the individual into normal class delivery of the curriculum. Other pupils often enjoy activities or games which may originally have been designed for an individual with special needs. The learning community of the classroom will support a wealth of diversity itself, if flexibly managed and democratically controlled. When pupils have joint purposes with teachers they can carry forward individuals whose needs may be quite great, and who on their own would struggle to make any progress (this theme is continued in *Chapter 5*).

Review resources regularly

Some pupils will have additional resources to help them access the curriculum. Some of these are technical in nature. Equipment must be kept in good condition, with spare parts and switches available. Pupils may need training to use this equipment efficiently – for example, keyboard skills may need to be taught by a suitable instructor. Staff will need training to use aids or to develop ICT activities. The teaching team, with the SENCo's help, should review 'packages' used with intervention groups and check that they are helping pupils make progress.

Concluding thoughts

The above sections have been included to give food for thought when planning SEN support or considering different ways of delivering the curriculum to motivate learning. Clearly, most curriculum planning and development of pedagogy and resources are issues for whole-school development. SENCos can use their particular skills and knowledge and their depth and breadth of understanding of curriculum issues to:

• draw attention to pupils' individual differences and abilities and needs, and build on their strengths, learning preferences and real-world experiences. Have high expectations for those with additional needs;
• remind colleagues that, for many pupils, the role of the teacher is to *mediate* learning so that the pupil makes connections between their previous experience and the new material;
• remind teachers that they should remain in charge of the curriculum delivery for those with additional needs and not leave this task to be carried out by TAs on their own;
• help the school to work proactively to meet the needs of pupils by being a change agent for curriculum planning.

This chapter has looked at both theoretical and practical issues related to the delivery of the whole curriculum. The SENCo's role in relation to helping colleagues with aspects of teaching and learning is to understand what potential barriers there might be for those with significant difficulties. This requires careful observation and assessment, not only of the individual pupils' strategies in learning, but also of the classroom environment in which they function. Their aim will be to equip all teachers with a range of appropriate strategies to meet the majority of needs. The pupils themselves will be able to give feedback to teachers regarding what helps them and what further support or change is needed.

CHAPTER 5

Managing Effective Support

Introduction and changing context

This chapter looks at the management of effective support and is in two parts. In the first part we answer the 'who, what, when, how and why' questions about managing support staff, most often teaching assistants (TAs), in a whole-school approach. In the second part we examine the SENCo's role and responsibilities in managing TAs and monitoring additional provision. We have used the term 'teaching assistants' to include learning support assistants and other assistants who support pupils with SEND.

What is SEN support?

In recent years, the management of support systems has become a central responsibility for SENCos and senior staff. Most pupils with SEN who have Statements or EHC plans, and many who do not, will have been allocated such support, provided by specialist teachers or external services or, more likely, by teaching assistants. The purpose of support for children and young people with SEND is to close, as far as is possible, the attainment gap between these children and their peers; to enable them to fulfil high expectations of their individual potential; to develop their independence; and to enable them to make a smooth transition through different stages of education towards an independent and confident adult life.

Who provides support?

The range of people who work alongside a class or subject teacher may include: TAs working with children with Statements or EHC plans; other TAs employed by the school; nursery nurses; learning mentors, therapists, support and specialist teachers on the school staff; peripatetic teachers/advisers from an LA service; special school teachers working in an outreach capacity; and volunteers or parents (see *Chapter 7*). Many schools employ Higher Level Teaching Assistants (HLTAs), who must demonstrate that they have met the professional standards established by the National College for Teaching and Leadership. HLTAs will have more demanding roles than TAs, often managing them or carrying out specialist work, including taking a class, under the supervision of a teacher.

For most students with SEN, support will be provided by teaching assistants employed by the school. Many TAs will have a 'pedagogical role' (Blatchford *et al.* 2012a), leading 'catch-up' programmes and other interventions and offering individual and group support in lessons. The issue for schools, of course, is how well TAs are enabled to do this.

Research into the deployment and impact of support staff

Recent extensive and rigorous research was undertaken on the deployment and impact of support staff (the DISS Report) (Blatchford *et al.* 2008). It identified critical issues about teaching assistants' current deployment (how TAs are used in schools), preparedness (how they are trained and prepared for their work) and practice (what they do with pupils), and the negative impact of TA support on pupil learning, which the authors described as 'troubling and unexpected' (Russell *et al.* 2013: 14). They emphasise that this is not the fault of TAs, who are valued by teachers for their contribution to classroom management. They found that TAs generally have a direct teaching role, routinely supporting lower-attaining pupils and pupils with SEN, for whom they have often become the primary educators. As a consequence of working with TAs one-to-one or in groups, often outside the classroom, pupils with SEN can be separated from the teacher, the curriculum and their peers. Such separation of pupils and teacher would not be considered appropriate for pupils without SEN or disabilities. Moreover, TAs often have limited subject knowledge and have been inadequately prepared for their teaching role. Time for teachers and TAs to plan, prepare lessons, share feedback and discuss the progress of pupils is often limited. Teachers are not generally trained to manage TAs, nor are they always well informed about how to meet special needs. Thus, teachers and TAs are often not well prepared for working together.

Teachers' and TAs' verbal interactions with pupils revealed significant differences. TAs often gave too much help, provided answers to their own questions and most frequently used closed (rather than open) questions. TAs were often more concerned with completion of tasks than whether pupils were learning, gaining understandings of concepts, thinking for themselves and becoming independent. However, when TAs had had training in teaching strategies and specific interventions, pupil progress was considerably better (Blatchford *et al.* 2012a).

Ofsted (2006) found that pupils in mainstream schools were less likely than those who had access to specialist teachers to make academic progress where support from TAs was the main provision. They stated that although TAs provide valuable support and undertake difficult roles, they should not be a substitute for focused, highly skilled teaching. In other words, TA support should be 'additional to' the teacher's work with the child, not an alternative to it.

The DISS research team recommended regular joint planning and greater flexibility in teacher and TA roles in the classroom, working with different individuals and groups. This change would ensure that teachers know more about their pupils with SEN and TAs working with more able pupils would have higher aspirations for pupils with

SEN. They also advocated training for TAs to improve verbal interactions, especially questioning skills. Research undertaken by the Education Endowment Foundation in 2013 (see EEF 2014) using two randomised controlled trials has provided a strong indication that, when trained and deployed carefully to support pupils one-to-one or in small groups through structured interventions in literacy and numeracy, teaching assistants can improve learning.

The DISS researchers state firmly and repeatedly that effective TA practice depends not on 'the decisions made by TAs but decisions made by school leaders about how TAs are used and prepared' (Webster and Blatchford 2013: 12). The research project on effective deployment of teaching assistants (EDTA) (Blatchford *et al.* 2012b) piloted new and successful ways of working. Many schools nationally are aiming to maximise the impact of teaching assistants on pupil progress and using practical advice born of research (Russell *et al.* 2013). The responsibility for effective support lies with school leaders implementing whole-school policies on the deployment, training and practice of teaching assistants and on monitoring the impact of such policies on teaching and on pupil progress. The SENCo, as a contributor to the wider leadership team, has an important strategic, management and organisational role in this.

Where does support take place?

There have been arguments that any form of support that does not take place within the classroom is against inclusive principles, resulting in a form of internal exclusion for certain pupils. This is too simplistic, as individual timetables can be carefully planned to be flexible, and good liaison and planning can help offset missed curricular activities. That said, as Russell *et al.* (2013) made clear, lessons outside the classroom increase the separation of children with SEN from their teachers and their peers. There is also concern about the effects of withdrawal on the pupil's self-image. Younger pupils rarely mind being taken out in a group because their need for extra attention may be greater. With older pupils, it will be best to negotiate with the pupil. Often a 'clinic' approach, or a short, targeted intervention for a specific purpose such as difficulty in spelling or reading, can result in self-referral and be effective for older pupils. Ofsted (2010) found that learning was better when children and young people were given a say in deciding the support they need at any particular time, including when they would like to be left alone, and the Code (2014) reinforces this. TAs and SENCos often become skilled interpreters of pupils' wishes, and advocates for them.

For certain activities, especially those requiring careful listening, the classroom environment is too noisy. In other cases, the group activity itself will be disruptive to the rest of the class. In some rooms, finding space for extra adults is a problem, and too many adults in a classroom is an extravagant use of resources. Sometimes support is better given on a one-to-one basis, away from the classroom, as when children require individual sessions for speech and language therapy or physiotherapy. These programmes are often designed by specialists and delivered by TAs, who may develop support specialisms on which they can lead in training and advising other TAs and teachers. However, small-group work within class may be just as effective, depending on space and classroom organisation.

Whether TAs and other support staff work within or outside the classroom, their role is to empower pupils to be as independent learners as possible. Pupils need time and opportunity to attempt tasks, make and learn from mistakes and develop autonomy. Overprotective support will stifle independence. Sessions must be carefully planned to enhance what is happening in class, and flexible timetabling will be needed so that pupils do not lose their curriculum entitlement, nor its breadth and balance.

It is inappropriate for support teaching to take place in corridors, school halls and other public places, where pupils have little chance to concentrate and may well be embarrassed. When lessons take place outside the classroom, schools must ensure that they reach the same high-quality teaching standards expected inside. This will require appropriate training for TAs in subject knowledge and teaching skills. Other staff will need training in observation, supervision and monitoring of support outside the classroom. Observation is best carried out by the SENCo with SLT, but classroom teachers, heads of departments, TAs and HLTAs may also gain from joint observations of teaching and learning for pupils with SEND.

Extra resourced provision

Sometimes schools establish resource centres, or units, where pupils with similar needs can be given extra support. Most frequently such units are for those with physical or sensory difficulties, autism or language and communication difficulties. In such provision, a group of pupils with similar disabilities is taught by specialist teachers with TA support. Pupils spend varying amounts of time in mainstream classes, often supported by TAs with close knowledge of their needs. Ofsted (2006) found that mainstream schools with extra resourced provision were particularly successful in achieving high outcomes for pupils with SEND academically, socially and personally. However, in 2010 they observed that no one model, whether a special school, full inclusion in a mainstream setting or a specialist unit co-located with a mainstream setting, worked better than any other in ensuring good provision for children with SEND (Ofsted, 2010). Pupils who have experienced different types of provision often report a strong preference for special schools or units. This is often because being the only child who has a certain disability, such as a hearing impairment, can be an isolating experience (MacConville *et al.* 2007).

The class or subject teacher's responsibility for effective support

The location for support need not be problematic, as long as there is access to high-quality teaching to ensure progress. The task of the SENCo is to keep inclusive principles at the forefront of everyone's mind when planning support and devising support timetables. This will mean ensuring that teachers and teaching assistants have the knowledge and skills to plan and teach a high-quality differentiated curriculum that meets the needs of pupils with a wide range of learning difficulties.

The importance of high-quality teaching

Whatever individual or group support is available, it cannot compensate for a poorly differentiated curriculum, low expectations and a lack of high-quality teaching. If the focus is solely on the child, rather than the curriculum content or classroom context, support may fail. Ofsted (2010) clearly identified poor-quality teaching as the reason for much underachievement being labelled as evidence of SEN within children. The SEND Code of Practice (DfE/DoH 2015: 6.37) states firmly that 'high quality differentiated teaching is the first step in responding to SEND and … no amount of support can compensate for its absence' (see *Chapter 4*).

'Teachers are responsible and accountable for the progress and development of the pupils in their class, including where pupils access support from teaching assistants or specialist staff' (DfE/DoH 2015: 6.36). Even when teaching pupils with SEND is devolved in practice to TAs, the graduated support structure in the Code expects teachers to take the principal responsibility to 'assess, plan, do and review' (DfE/DoH 2015: 6.44–6.56), with the SENCo as consultant and support. This means that whether or not a TA is involved in working with a pupil, it remains the teacher's responsibility to plan high-quality teaching with the TA, respond to TA feedback and monitor progress. Most importantly, the teacher must ensure that what the pupil has learned outside the classroom is reflected, rehearsed and reinforced within it, so that the responsibility for making the links between the intervention and the classroom learning is not left to the pupil.

Planning ahead

TAs should be assured of lesson plans in advance and be given a clear structure to their classroom work and time for preparation of any resources. Gerschel (2005) and Russell *et al.* (2013) found that TAs are frequently asked to modify and interpret teaching in a lesson, often without prior notice of what is being taught. Although innovative ideas may be generated 'on the spot', curriculum goals and learning objectives must be made clear to TAs in advance of the lesson. Better preparedness for teachers and TAs, Russell *et al.* (2013) argue, comes with better training for teachers to manage TAs, better induction for TAs, clarity of expectations, more training for TAs in subject and pedagogic knowledge and skills, and more timetabled opportunities for teachers and TAs to plan and review pupil progress together.

The SENCo's role in managing support

Line management and performance management

For effective management there should be 'a viable organisational structure within the school with clearly defined roles and responsibilities for TAs and their managers, including the SENCO and the teaching staff with whom they work' (Gerschel 2005: 70). SENCos clearly have a role in improving what Blatchford *et al.* (2012a) called deployment, preparedness and practice. They may also line-manage TAs with responsibility for supporting pupils with SEND. There is occasionally an uncomfortable hiatus between teachers' management responsibilities for what the TA does in the classroom and the overall line-management responsibilities of the SENCo for ensuring appropriate provision for pupils with SEND. Sometimes different 'types' of TA (e.g. general classroom support, support for pupils with EAL) have different line managers. Consistent expectations and coherent practice for all TAs need to be discussed and resolved at a whole-school level for policy and an individual level for practice. TAs supporting SEND will need to meet regularly with the SENCo to discuss their work individually and as a group (Gerschel 2005). Arrangements for review of TA work (performance management) need to be explicit. SENCos may find themselves undertaking this. It will require observation of TAs at work and thoughtful discussion of how TAs' strengths can be used most effectively and areas for improvement addressed. Self-reviews by TAs can help to identify these areas. SENCOs may organise observations of lessons with teachers and senior staff, and peer observations by other TAs or HLTAs.

Recruitment and job descriptions

Most schools now insist on at least basic-level literacy and numeracy qualifications for all TAs, although it is not unusual for TAs to be graduates spending time in the classroom before teacher training. SENCos will often be involved in the recruitment and appointment of TAs and may look for specialist skills or knowledge and/or a capacity to undertake training. Job descriptions for TAs should clearly define their roles and responsibilities and indicate how they will be supported and their work managed and reviewed. Job descriptions for TAs are often prepared by local authorities. They may be comprehensive and generic to the support role, but may also include a section recording the specific responsibilities of individual TAs, who often take on quite different roles. TAs may also contribute to their production. Balshaw and Farrell (2002) offer interesting models.

The National Occupational Standards for Supporting Teaching and Learning in schools (NOS for STL) (TDAS 2010) are overseen by the National College for Teaching and Leadership. NOS for STL/TA describe what TAs need to do, know and understand in their roles through a wide range of units, and can be used selectively for recruitment, job descriptions and training and development. The units link up with the Qualifications and Credit Framework (QCF 2013), and a range of further qualifications for TAs, up to foundation degree level, is available. TAs should have opportunities for personal and professional skills development.

Induction and training

SENCos will often have responsibility for the induction and training of TAs. Induction programmes should involve an introduction to essential systems, policies and practices within the school, including:

• SEN and disability;
• principles of teaching and learning;
• key issues about managing behaviour and enhancing self-esteem;
• communication processes with teachers, parents and pupils;
• key principles of equality policy;
• health and safety issues, including manual handling of pupils with SEND.

As part of induction, there should be opportunities for new TAs to shadow more experienced TAs. Balshaw (1999) suggests that induction should include the development of a consistency of approach towards positive provision and establishment of ground rules for each staff or classroom team. Certainly, all TAs should know what is expected of them regarding:

• teaching and learning;
• any specialist practice or care relating to individual pupils with SEND;
• behaviour management, rewards and sanctions;
• record-keeping and feedback;
• contributions to assessment and reviews;
• marking;
• pupil voice and advocacy;
• contact with parents.

The SENCo has an important role in supporting, advising and training teachers and TAs to ensure that they have the skills and knowledge to carry out their combined and separate planning and teaching roles. Teachers need to learn about effective management and deployment of TAs; Ofsted are averse to seeing TAs simply 'listening to the teacher' or 'Velcro-ed' to pupils (Gerschel 2005). TAs need to be prepared for their contributions to reviews of pupil progress, including Annual Reviews of EHCPs or Statements. Regular short training sessions should inform TAs about the work of therapists and other professionals and should extend their knowledge of different types of special needs and effective support (Gerschel 2005). Russell *et al.* (2013) suggest that some things developed for TAs may also be applicable to teachers; they may also want a structured programme to inform and enskill them, particularly in the light of the specific responsibilities reinforced in the SEND Code of Practice (DfE/DoH 2015). It may be beneficial to train TAs and teachers together so that policies and practices for support move forward in a coherent manner. Such training could address high-frequency special needs likely to occur in every school, such as speech, language and communication needs; autistic spectrum difficulties; dyslexia; and common individual conditions such as cerebral palsy, Down's syndrome or mental health issues (see *Source List* and *Chapter 11*).

The SENCo needs to support the practice of TAs, to ensure that they are more confident in how to teach proactively with a strong knowledge base so that they are not limited to reactive responses to pupils' needs. They also need to be less focused on task completion and more aware of how to teach for understanding (Ofsted 2010). Training on, for example, questioning skills and metacognitive approaches to learning has been seen to make a significant difference to TAs' practice and impact (Russell *et al.* 2013). Successful strategies can also be taught: rehearsing prerequisite skills and concepts with pupils before a lesson is often very helpful. Specialist materials can also be produced by TAs, if they are given appropriate direction and the time to produce resources.

Improving whole-school practice

Liaison time

Adequate time for teachers and TAs to liaise over lesson plans, discuss teaching strategies, share feedback and review pupils' progress has emerged as essential to effective support for pupils. Schools have found practical and creative solutions to enable this regular liaison to take place, including using assemblies and specialist lessons such as PE or music, and employing TAs for longer or more varied hours.

Liaison time is sometimes not seen as a priority by senior management, but it has certainly been seen as a key factor in collaboration between teachers and TAs for the past two decades. The Audit Commission (1992) pointed out that if a small amount of the time spent alongside pupils was redirected into planning and discussion about individual pupils between supporting adults and classroom teachers, there would be a significant improvement in effectiveness. Ofsted (1996: 5) stated that the most influential factor in the effectiveness of in-class support is the quality of joint planning of the work between class/subject teacher and the support teacher or assistant. Some schools monitor the use and impact of liaison time in building teaching partnerships, enabling effective planning and review and improving pupils' progress, and find it to be cost-effective.

Developing collaborative cultures

Support can take the form of collaborative partnerships where two adults plan and deliver aspects of the subject and where good use of group work is possible. Most commonly, teachers and TAs work together, sometimes alternating their teaching roles with different pupils. A collaborative culture will be evident to pupils and will support teaching and model learning. The classroom context affects children's individual responses to learning (see *Chapter 4*). Hart (1995) argues that differentiating the curriculum to meet individual needs must reflect that individual differences are, in part, the products of school and classroom processes. When teachers modify these processes for individuals, they are making 'reasonable adjustments'.

By working together and talking about teaching and learning, adults can help each other make sense of the complexity of the classroom environment. Successful teams will take time to analyse the various elements of classroom interactions and evaluate how support can best address the various challenges that arise. Balshaw (1999) refers to research on teachers and TAs working together in 'learning partnerships' to support and challenge each other.

Within the collaborative classroom, the SENCo may act in the role of support teacher, team-teacher or model, as a means of helping develop good practice. It is the SENCo's role 'to support the class or subject teacher in the further assessment of the child's strengths and weaknesses and in problem-solving and advising on the effective implementation of support' (DfE/DoH 2015: 6.52).

Evaluating interventions and the impact of support

The SENCo, with the class or subject teacher, must evaluate the success and impact of the TA-led interventions and monitor the progress of pupils with SEND. Consequently, SENCos and teachers must ensure that TAs understand targets and intended learning outcomes, as well as how to enable pupils to meet them. The indicators used to judge the effectiveness and impact of interventions must be robust and clear. They should state the expected outcomes of the intervention, so that actual outcomes can be measured against them. Interventions that are not effective in achieving their intended outcomes should be ceased. Funding, such as the Pupil Premium, may have a significant impact on the population of pupils with SEND, and SENCos are often expected to advise on how it would be best spent. There is now a considerable body of research evidence from universities, educational organisations and charities, such as the Educational Endowment Foundation, to inform teachers of what works in raising attainment, and SENCos should refer to this. To monitor the success of support and its relationship to pupil progress, SENCos should ask:

- How well is this intervention/support strategy helping pupils to achieve their targets?
- How do I know?
- What evidence of progress is there?

This is particularly important at a time when value for money must be taken into account.

SENCos should have regular oversight of the planning undertaken by teachers and TAs and should observe teaching for pupils with SEND both by TAs and teachers, including the use made of TAs to maximise their impact in the classroom. This may be best achieved by the SENCo working with the SLT. Ofsted inspectors expect all teachers to plan appropriately for all pupils, including those with SEN, and their judgements reflect the value that TAs add to the classroom and the progress of pupils with SEND (Ofsted 2014). They are looking for TA impact, not merely presence.

Developing and reviewing support policies and practice

This chapter has considered how to make support more effective. It has focused particularly on the role of TAs. SENCos have a role in explaining the importance of these issues to the SLT and governors; if not addressed, valuable resources may be wasted or not used efficiently enough for the benefit of the pupils. Russell *et al.* (2013) offer invaluable advice on effective management of TAs to maximise their impact. The investment of time in good SENCo management practice will be repaid in better quality support, confident staff and increased pupil progress (see *Activity 4* – An Organisational Checklist).

Auditing what is working in support

It is helpful to audit what is or is not working in support. In *Activity 3* we have provided an extensive Audit of Support Policy and Practice which you can use or adapt to identify the areas of your school's current policy and practice which are working well and/or which could be improved. It will help you to identify any discrepancies between the ideal and the reality, in policy and practice. It can be used with all staff or with specific groups to trigger discussion on how support can be made most effective. This chapter will help to address issues raised.

Chapter 6

Working with Parents, Children and Young People

The theme of involving children, young people and parents is introduced in the first chapter of the SEND Code of Practice (DfE/DoH 2015), and runs through all subsequent chapters. The emphasis is on consultation and effective participation in decision-making. The Code says that all partners – education, health and social care – must improve services in the light of the views of parents, children and young people. Stobbs (2014a) also describes the changing emphasis within the Children and Families Act (2014) on parents' participation as key participants in decision-making. She points out that to be effective, parents must have access to accurate and impartial information and support; as she also says, this must be founded on good communication, based on trust. Schools will be expected to meet parents with SEND at least three times a year. It will be important to develop listening skills, so that parents' views are understood, as effective engagement of parents has a beneficial impact on children's progress. The Code continues to emphasise the importance of child views, but it extends this to young people up to the age of 25, if they have an EHC plan. This chapter looks at how schools and their SENCo can:

• work effectively with children and young people to learn about their views, feelings and wishes;
• work with parents/carers to build good partnerships which improve pupil well-being and progress;
• consider how the views of young people should be used when planning for their support.

Each section will look both at the personal skills of the SENCo and teachers and at features of the whole-school approach.

Everyone looks to the SENCo for support, advice and even counselling, but for this to be effective a number of factors must be in place, one of which is the SENCo's own feeling of confidence. This will be stronger when based on a feeling of competence built up through knowledge and skills gained from experience and training. It takes time to build up this confidence and competence so as to be in a position to support others and act as a change agent in a school. Another factor will be how effectively the school, as a whole, works with parents and their children. This should be an area of school policy and practice which is regularly reviewed and improved.

The early years

It is important to recognise that taking account of the child's feelings and preferences should start as young as possible. In the beginning, their views will be represented by those who work closely with them, mainly through observations in different settings. One of the best ways of getting some idea of a very young child's perspective is through good observation, especially if this is across a variety of activities with different adults. The observer can note levels of participation in an activity, signs of enjoyment or distress and interaction with other children and adults. Observations need to be carefully recorded and interpreted. Parents' observations in the home setting and over time can be added to those in the Early Years setting. Sharing these types of observations with parents and other staff can build up a picture of the child and help to frame questions about identification of needs and ways to support them.

Multi-professional teamwork and the key worker

Since 2003 and the Every Child Matters agenda, more co-ordinated methods of working with families have been developed. This was necessary because tragic cases showed up how fragmented services were in their working practices, with this sometimes resulting in the loss of vital information. One aspect of these new professional practices was the introduction of the 'key worker' concept. As Roffey and Parry (2013) explain, the idea was to avoid 'help fatigue' for parents who had too many visitors to their home, providing confusing information or leading to information overload. The key worker also gives emotional and practical support, and builds a relationship with the family. Importantly, the key worker also co-ordinates services and helps with planning, as well as acting as an advocate for the child (see *Chapter 7* for more on the team around the child).

When a child with SEND enters Early Years provision, it may be the first time that anyone has shown a concern. Within the home environment, the parent may not have noticed anything to worry them. Parents can sometimes be reluctant to recognise that their child has a difficulty or disability. This can be for a number of reasons. They may have little experience of other children, or of child development norms. They may be afraid of labelling and rejection, or of loss of face within the family. They may prefer to take a 'wait and see' approach. In such cases, keeping up a dialogue is important – parents must be given time and opportunities to share their own views with key staff, over weeks if necessary. The way in which a child is described to their parents is very important and it is essential to use positive language. Building a true partnership requires mutual respect and an ability to listen to the views of others and to record these carefully. When parents first meet professionals, they may feel overwhelmed by the knowledge and expertise of these people but, in reality, it is the parent who is the expert on the subject of their own child.

Learning to be a skilled observer

Learning observation skills gives teachers a useful tool for assessment and general problem-solving. Observation can be for set times (e.g. ten minutes) or of specific events or a specific context, such as the playground. Starting the observation without a precise focus may be possible, but increasingly focusing on an intended feature may give more insight. If pupil perspectives are the focus, this may need to be combined with interview techniques.

A number of observation techniques are given in *Appendix 6a*. Accurate observation for as little as ten minutes, if focused and prepared, can give insights into a particular area of concern, whether for an individual pupil or for a group. Always remember that observation will be affected by bias, so if more than one adult can observe to a prepared schedule, the results may be more reliable.

School-aged children

Achieving an understanding of the pupil's own view of their school experience and their educational needs requires the teacher to have the ability to change perspective. Teachers have to let go of their position of authority for a short time and view the world of the classroom from the pupil's point of view. This may best be done through becoming a careful observer of certain times and taking detailed notes. If someone else can manage the class for a short session while this observation takes place, it will be easier for the teacher to be free to observe.

Using other techniques to gain pupils' views

Another way to gain a child's perspective is, of course, to ask the pupil to talk about or express their views. This can be through direct questions about an aspect of their work such as reading or homework, or it can be through more open-ended questioning about school or friends. Open-ended interviewing is difficult for some teachers to do, partly because of time constraints and partly because it is a skill to be learnt. Sometimes other adults – TAs or support professionals – may fare better because they may offer less threat to pupils or have time to see pupils in a more relaxed environment. The whole class can be given exercises to evaluate an aspect of their own learning, possibly to rate how confident they feel about various aspects of their learning. For younger pupils, faces with different expressions can be used to rate answers instead of words (see *Appendix 6b*).

It is more difficult to gain a view of pupil perspective where the pupil lacks the language to express their thoughts and feelings in words. In these cases, observations from more than one adult may need to be combined to give a feel for the pupil's perspective. This can be achieved by looking at pupil reactions to activities, teaching approaches and at resources and events. Ancillary helpers' and parents' observations about different aspects of the pupil's development and feelings of self-worth are very helpful in putting together a joint perspective. The use of video cameras and tape recorders can help collect valuable data in cases where more direct questioning is difficult – for example, with the developmentally young or pupils with language impairment. These would not be kept as a long-term record, but might help analyse complex observations. The issue of parental permission for video use has become increasingly important. Some schools ensure that such permission is obtained for pedagogical purposes when the pupil is admitted to the school. Drawings and symbolic representations of situations as perceived during play can all add to the teacher's understanding of pupil perspectives.

The above approaches take time, even for just one child, and cannot be used for all the pupils in a class or on the SEN register. Different methods can be selected for different children and at different times. It is useful however if, as an aspect of training sessions, teachers can practise some of the skills required in collecting and collating information. This will enhance their ability to look at pupil perspectives. For some teachers, the exercise of *really* trying to understand one pupil, from a child's point of view, is a revelation.

Involving children in the 'Assess, Plan, Do, Review' process

As the child gets older, in the primary and (particularly) the secondary school, the child's own views can, to an increasing extent, be collected through interviews as well as observation. Children require practice in evaluating their learning environment and their progress, and expressing their evaluations so that they can be understood. The value of meta-cognitive approaches – learning to learn – has already been discussed (in *Chapter 4*). Children need to be helped to develop self-regulatory strategies, and to take control over their own learning. Part of SEN support will be to build up these strategies, and to aim for independence; being able to know when to ask for help and when to treat a task as a challenge, to be tried alone.

Children will also need to be supported in target-setting and reviewing, as part of the 'Assess, Plan, Do, Review' cycle. Friswell (2014:10) says that 'The challenge for us as teachers is to consider how, in the day-to-day classroom experience, we support pupils to gain a better awareness of the way they learn best'.

Pupil views can be included in the discussion at the review meeting, but it may be preferable for these to be gathered in advance, as part of the preparation. Helping all children to develop as independent learners should be a whole-school goal, not one confined to SEND policy. Training will be needed for both teachers and TAs, to develop knowledge and skills related to this aspect of teaching and learning. Monitoring the growth of such learning skills and independence should be part of what is recorded.

School policy – taking pupil perspectives into account

In line with the United Nations Convention on the Rights of the Child (Articles 12 and 13) (United Nations 1989), the new Code is explicit that children and young people must be part of the decision-making process with regard to all aspects of their learning, insofar as this is possible. They have a unique knowledge of their needs, and their views should be listened to and taken into account. The law has strengthened pupils' rights to be involved in decision-making and planning meetings, such as reviews of Statements or EHC plans. However, teachers may still find it difficult to be sure that they have heard the 'true pupil voice'. Regular conferencing times at which the pupils' views are taken down can be built into review procedures or provided for all pupils. As part of the review of the SEN policy, the following questions need to be asked:

• Do we take account of pupils' viewpoints and perspectives?
• Do we have procedures and times when we can note pupils' viewpoints and perspectives?
• Do pupils' views and perspectives influence policy-making in the school?
• Do we seek the views of pupils with a range of SEND?

In some schools, it is expected that all units of teaching and learning will include some opportunities for pupil feedback not only on what they have learnt, but also on what teaching approaches were most successful.

SENCos need to be aware, when considering the pupil voice, of the disproportionate number of pupils with SEN who are excluded permanently or for a fixed term. Schools and their SENCos need to work closely with pupils at risk of exclusion and their families to take preventative steps and, in the event that it is necessary, to give an account of all the support that was given and why it failed.

Involving parents in planning and reviewing progress

The SEND Code of Practice (DfE/DoH 2015: 6.64–6.71) gives details of how schools should work with parents when reviewing their child's progress. Regular meetings can provide information about the success of SEN support as seen from the parents' and child's viewpoints. The Code indicates that discussions of this kind require knowledge of the pupil and skill on the part of the teacher – usually this will be the class teacher or form teacher, supported by the SENCo. Training for this may be required, as will sufficient time for meetings. A record of the meeting and its agreed outcomes should be made, shared with appropriate school staff and given to the pupil's parents.

The structured conversation

The Achievement for All (DCSF 2009c) project introduced the 'structured conversation' as a means to improve engagement with parents. The framework for a structured conversation has four steps:

• *Explore* – this requires the Key Teacher to actively listen to the parent, and to be able to paraphrase their key points and feelings in order to understand their viewpoints. Questions need to be tentative in tone, and should facilitate what the parent wants to say.
• *Focus* – This step is used to identify priorities, and to clarify parents' key issues.

- *Plan* – Targets are agreed between the Key Teacher and the parent. A target is a prediction plus a challenge. They should be outcome-focused (see *Chapter 3*).
- *Review* – This is where the teacher summarises what has been covered, agrees the next steps with the parent and arranges for future communication.

The structured conversation techniques can be applied to working with parents when using the Code's 'graduated approach' of 'Assess, Plan, Do, Review'. In preparation for the meeting with parent(s), the Key Teacher gathers information about their child from assessments (formal or informal), the points of view of other members of staff and, of course, the pupil's own views. This information, although available, will not be considered as a first step at the meeting, because it is more important to find out the parents' perspectives. However, some information will need to be shared in order to agree on priorities and to set targets. When the review takes place, the parent should be present if possible. If the original meeting took an outcomes approach, it will be easier to see whether these have been achieved.

Developing listening skills

To carry out the above conversations it will be necessary to understand the parents' viewpoint, which will require a change of perspective for teachers. If a true partnership with parents is to be established, then the teacher or the SENCo needs to learn to listen to and value the parents' expertise about their own child or their concerns about his or her progress. (In linguistically diverse schools and communities, parents may need an interpreter.) To do this effectively, it is necessary to learn new skills. Teachers are good at expressing themselves and activating ideas; they may not be quite as good as listeners. Listening effectively in the consultative role is a skill to be learnt and practised.

Empathic listening

In this mode, the listener obeys certain ground rules. These are:

- keep eye contact;
- keep still, do not distract your listener by fiddling with pens, etc.;
- keep your own comments to a minimum, such as 'I see', 'right', 'I understand' and 'yes';
- if longer comments are required, make these reflective, i.e. feedback the main point as you understood it, so it can be checked; use these comments to summarise points and check that you have understood what was said;
- don't be afraid to feed back feelings as well as facts: 'That must have made you angry', 'You were upset by. . .'.

Such listening sessions will need time limits, which should be set in advance if possible: 'We've got half an hour, please tell me your concerns and worries, we will try to find some answers.' Check that the parent is happy for you to take notes. Often it is not a good idea to do this if you are really trying to listen, as you cannot keep eye contact and write. It may be a good idea to make time to summarise at the end of the session and agree a few points which can be written down. Establishing a feeling of trust is more important than note-taking at this point. Once the problem has been identified and the parent feels they have been listened to, it is possible to move into *problem-solving mode*.

Problem-solving

As a first step, this requires that the problem has been clearly identified. Next, actions can be jointly planned with the parent to try to solve the problem. Problem-solving again needs a sensitive approach from the teacher, while setting boundaries for what is achievable in school within limited resources. Wherever possible, the parents/carers will feel more like a partner if they can suggest ideas to be discussed, and can perhaps offer to help in some way at home or in school. Joint targets or outcomes can then be decided and a date to review progress made. Copies of written notes of meetings should be given to parents wherever possible.

Cultural awareness

Families and communities have different attitudes to having a child with SEND; some may be 'in denial', or feel ashamed. Cultural differences will need to be recognised and everyone involved should be sensitive to these. Experienced staff should be consulted if there is uncertainty regarding how to interact in the child's best interests. If interpreters are used they should be helped to understand the language and concept of SEN.

Developing partnerships

If schools have listened to parents when developing other policies, then parents' perspectives will already be reflected. Parents of pupils with SEN are, however, particularly vulnerable: some parents are not always confident enough to ask for their views to be taken into account, or may not even know their rights. It is therefore essential that the SENCo gives parents information about these rights. Parents need to have the graduated assessment procedure explained. They need to know about LA services which may be called upon to support their child. School provision for SEN also needs to be explained (see *Appendix 2a* and *Chapter 7*).

Parents may sometimes have feelings of anger, guilt and frustration in finding that their child is not making the expected progress. Making a partnership with such parents requires the SENCo to have skills of assertiveness and the ability to set limits, in particular regarding how to manage time. If the relationship is not dealt with carefully, a confrontation rather than a partnership can occur. As Dale (1996) explains, parents can go through a 'psychic shock' when they first hear of their child's disability. The first phase may only last a day or so, at which time they need sympathy and understanding. Next, information is required to help them orientate. The following step will be to use a problem-solving approach to help parents come to terms with the new situation. Empathic listening can still help to establish a rapport, and can be followed by a structured problem-solving session. If the parents feel they really have been listened to and their viewpoints have been taken into account, they will feel calmer and more able to look for joint practical solutions. If, however, their feelings seem irrational and solutions are beyond the resources of the school, it may be necessary to seek help either from other members of the school – the head, for example – or outside professionals.

Almost all parents can be brought into a partnership situation. Difficulties arise when promises are broken, resources do not arrive, the pupil is absent intermittently or for long periods or staff are inconsistent in following the school's SEN policy. In many of these cases, the teacher's ability to work in partnership with parents dwindles. Parents' own needs cannot fully be addressed by the school, but it is possible to get a personal referral for help. Some SENCos have found that setting up parent support groups within the school has enabled parents to share expertise and develop skills. Such groups are sometimes facilitated by outside parenting skills trainers. The questions SENCos need to keep in mind when working with parents are:

- What is a possible outcome of this meeting which will benefit the child?
- What resources are available from the school or the community to support this child and parent?
- What is achievable in the immediate future, and in the more distant future?

Summarising the answers to these questions and feeding back to the parents in a positive manner is a way of recording the meeting.

Developing policy for working with parents

Parents are defined under the Children Act (1989) as those who have parental responsibility for the child or who have care of the child (full description in *Appendix 6c*). The school's policy should contain a clear statement of the arrangements for ensuring close working partnerships with parents/carers of children with special educational needs. This will mean incorporating parents' views in assessment and reviews and ensuring parents are fully informed about the school's procedures and are made welcome in the school. Much of this will be achieved if a policy for parents of all pupils is inclusive and enhances participation. SEN policy should not be an add-on, but an integral part of the school's general way of working with parents.

The Equality Act (2010) requires schools to consult with parents of pupils with SEND and parents who themselves have disabilities. They must also consult with pupils, staff, governors and other stakeholders about the impact all school policies and practices have on those with SEND, and how improvements could be made. The process and outcomes of such consultation must be produced as Equality Objectives and an action plan. Part of SEN policy planning will be to work out how key teachers can provide sufficient allocated time for meetings with parents of children with more complex needs.

Communication of information

Wherever possible, parents should give permission for information to be shared with appropriate others. Their permission is also needed if requests are made to other professionals, such as those from the health services. However, some information about individual preferences and support may be essential for the child's well-being. SENCos need to plan for particular staffing situations, such as:

- supply teachers and temporary or new staff, who need basic and necessary information, given in a quick, accessible briefing which can prevent the child being faced with unhappy events;
- playground supervisors, who may need some training about types of special needs and their effects on behaviour in a playground.

All of this should be part of the whole-school approach to meeting all children's needs, but those with certain disabilities may require more careful attention. (See also DfE/DoH 2015: 9.32–9.34 on sharing information.)

Young people's views

The young disabled in school

It is essential to recognise that the young disabled person may very well wish to deny their disability in order to fit in and feel 'normal' within their peer group. Allan (1999) explores this in great depth in her case studies of 11 young people with SEND aged 12 to 17 who attended mainstream schools, some with attached special units. Certain young people refused to use aids that had been supplied to help them, such as white canes for the visually impaired and hearing aids for the deaf. They also played down the consequences of denial when with their peer group, developing tactics such as laughter to defuse situations. Allan also describes the mainstream peer group's reactions to their disabled classmates, showing how important this is to social acceptance. Young people often do not want a 'fuss' to be made. They may not want their TA to support them in too obvious a way. This may present a problem if support is given in a way that is against the young person's wishes.

MacConville's emancipatory research

MacConville *et al.* (2007) and colleagues from the Ealing Specialist Support Team carried out what has been called 'emancipatory research' to give young disabled pupils a real voice. Members of the Specialist Support Team wrote chapters about the children and young people they supported in mainstream schools, and their viewpoints. Case studies of pupils with autistic spectrum disorder, visual impairment, hearing impairment, specific learning difficulties and physical difficulties are described, along with practical examples of what schools can do to help based on what young people have told the team members. Peer attitude is a frequent theme, along with descriptions of teacher attitudes and practices which help or hinder the self-esteem of these pupils. The pupils tell of humiliations caused both by peers and by teaching staff. MacConville points out that those who feel confident about themselves achieve higher academic results and have fewer behavioural problems, adding that listening to pupils' perspectives is a skilled task for which a knowledge of child development is important – in particular, knowledge of the development of self-esteem within social and emotional development. Her team based their work on the Cycle of Social and Emotional Development, which can become part of everyday school life (see *Source List*).

Young people at college

From the age of 16, young people are expected to take an active part in their reviews and in decision-making about support and outcomes. They need access to information, so that options and the consequences of choices can be discussed. Carr (2014) reports views expressed by young people from the consultative group set up by the Council for Disabled Children to advise the government on the draft Code of Practice. Some young people gave their views about taking more control at 16, saying that they felt unprepared to make such decisions and that they needed better information so that the consequences of decisions were clearer. Others were concerned about confidentiality, particularly in relation to aspects of their EHC plans. They thought that some parts should only be accessible on a need-to-know basis.

The SEND Code of Practice (DfE/DoH 2015) incorporated some of these points, saying:

> Young people must have confidence that they are receiving confidential and impartial information, advice and support. Staff working directly with young people should be trained to support them and work in partnership with them, enabling them to participate fully in decisions about the outcomes they wish to achieve. Young people may be finding their voice for the first time, and may need support in exercising choice and control over the support they receive including support and advice to take up and manage a Personal Budget.
>
> (DfE/DoH 2015: 2.15)

Mental capacity

Young people over compulsory school age have been given the right to make decisions about their provision. In most cases, the young person with a disability will still wish for a parent to be present at meetings where decisions are made, to help them with these decisions. In cases where the mental capacity of the young person may be insufficient, decisions can be made by a representative – probably their parent. Key principles around this issue are laid out in Annex 1 of the Code of Practice (2015) (DfE/DoH 2015). It points out that as much help and support as possible should be given, to enable the young person to express their views. It may be that, if they are helped to understand the information, they will be able to make the relevant decisions themselves.

College support

SEN support at college should always be discussed with the young person. Plans should be developed with the student. 'The support and intervention provided should meet the student's aspirations, and should be based on reliable evidence of effectiveness, and provided by practitioners with relevant skills and knowledge' (DfE/DoH 2015: 7.16).

Colleges should keep a student's records up to date, and inform students of their progress at regular intervals. Preparing students for adulthood is a theme developed further in *Chapter 8.*

Challenges for the SENCo in developing school policy and practice

The importance of working with parents and considering child views has always been central to the SENCo role, so what new challenges does the Children and Families Act (2014) bring? The emphasis on parents as decision-makers is now much greater than it was. For this to be effective, parents must have access to 'accurate and impartial' information (see 'Local Offer' in *Chapter 7*). Parents, children and young people should also be part of consultations on school policy and their views should be taken into account. Parental choice for their child has to be balanced with what is a fair allocation of resources to meet the needs of all pupils. This is why working with parents must be part of the whole-school approach, and should certainly not be confined to the SENCo role. The SENCo may, however, be able to highlight areas for staff and policy development, and be an advocate for children and young people who have SEND and their families.

CHAPTER 7

Working with Professionals and Organisations beyond the School

This chapter will focus on schools and their SENCos working with the range of services available locally, including the voluntary sector. The SEND Code of Practice (DfE/DoH 2015) brings together education, health and social care in closer co-operation in commissioning services for children and young people with SEND, some of whom will have an Education, Health and Care plan. This chapter will also try to help SENCos and their schools by explaining in detail how governors or proprietors involve other bodies, including health and social services, local authority support services and voluntary organisations, in meeting the needs of pupils with SEN and in supporting families of such pupils.

The Children and Families Act (2014) reforms include the introduction of the Local Offer (LO). There is a duty within the Act for the local authority (LA) to publish, in one place, details of all the services and provision available locally. This includes universal elements, such as schools, colleges and Early Years settings. Also included are other services provided by education and services provided by health and social care. The LO is not just a directory of services; it should include advice on how to access these services or to ask for an EHC assessment.

Information about these services will be available though the local authority's Local Offer (LO), which must be published accessibly in one place and regularly reviewed. The school's SEN Information Report (see *Appendix 2a*) must include references to how and when such specialist services are commissioned, and to the referral process. The main purpose of the LO is to provide information about provision, services and procedures available in the local district to parents/carers and young people in an accessible form. A parent must always be informed when outside agencies are involved with the assessment of their child, and should be helped to understand the process and to interpret the outcomes.

Familiarity with what is available in their local area has always been an important aspect of the SENCo's role. The second Code of Practice (2001) (DfES 2001b) listed possible services as specialist teachers of pupils with hearing, visual and speech and language impairments; teachers providing more general learning and behaviour support services; counsellors; educational psychologists; and advisers or teachers with knowledge of information technology for children with special educational needs. Since this was written, much has changed in what is available from LAs. Some services may no longer exist; some may be bought in by schools. This is one reason why it is necessary for the Local Offer to explain what services are available in each local authority, as each LA may be different. The LO is also the result of reviews as such as the Lamb Inquiry (DCFS 2009a), which reported parents' difficulties in finding out about local provision for SEN. In order to make the provision more responsive to needs, parents and young people are to be involved in the LO development and revision, and as Robertson (2013) comments, SENCos and the schools they work in will also have a major stake in its development.

Early Years services

The services available to parents/carers and their children from 0 to 5 should be explained in the LO. These are likely to include childminders and Early Years settings, as well as services such as Portage, speech and language therapy and specialised playgroups. Where there are additional concerns – about safeguarding, in particular – a Team Around the Child (TAC) approach may be used. TAC is a multi-disciplinary team, established on a case-by-case basis, to support the child and family. These teams aim to provide a joined-up approach. with the lead professional's intention to keep the child and family central to the process. Such teams require additional knowledge and skills, as compared to those who work in a single agency or independently. Staff must understand the roles and responsibilities of those working in different contexts to their own.

Other services

The LO should provide advice on access to apprenticeships and training opportunities, moving toward adulthood and independent living. It will list mediation services and explain how to deal with complaints or referrals to the SEND Tribunal. The full requirements of the LO are listed in the Special Educational Needs and Disability Regulations Schedule 2 Regulation 53, which is part of the Children and Families Act (2014). Detailed explanations are provided in Chapter 4 of the SEND Code of Practice (DfE/DoH 2015) and Pathfinder case studies.

Education services

The local authority has a range of duties, which include:

- ensuring sufficient provision for pupils with SEN and reviewing it annually;
- making arrangements for the statutory assessment of pupils and maintaining and reviewing EHC Plans, keeping to statutory time scales;

- publishing information on SEN funding and provision;
- monitoring the progress of children with SEN;
- making joint commissioning arrangements for education, health and care provision for children and young people with SEN or disabilities (Section 26 of the Act);
- managing the Local Offer (LO): providing information, support, advice and guidance to parents of children with SEN, including the provision of a statutory Parent Partnership Service and Mediation Service. Making sure complaints are dealt with effectively (see Pathfinder Information packs for more detail: www.sendpathfinder. co.uk/infopacks/).

Local Authorities' duties in co-ordinating an EHC plan

The principles of this are set out in Chapter 9 of the SEND Code of Practice (DfE/DoH 2015: 9.20–9.30). LAs must consult the child and child's parents, or the young person, through the process and production of the EHC Plan by:

- focusing on the child or young person as an individual;
- allowing the child and child's parents, or the young person, to express their views, wishes and feelings;
- enabling the child and child's parents, or the young person, to be part of the decision-making process.

This is described as a person-centred approach. Information and time must be provided for meetings and for meeting preparation. Advocates can be used where necessary. Such an advocate could be a family member or a member of a voluntary organisation (see *Chapter 9* for more).

Special schools

The LA will list all special schools and available resourced provision in mainstream schools. Some special schools share expertise with other schools, acting as an outreach service. Ofsted (2006) found that special schools had a particular strength in carefully matching the skills and interest of staff to the needs of groups of pupils, but teachers in mainstream schools had a better knowledge of individual subjects in the National Curriculum. There is therefore scope for further sharing of expertise and collaborative arrangements (see Tutt 2007 for case studies).

Educational Psychological Services (EPS)

Each LA in England has access to a community Educational Psychological Service (EPS). Trained psychologists work with children and young people in their schools and settings; they may also visit homes. Some EPSs may work a 'patch' system, looking after a cluster of schools on a regular basis, or be part of a multi-disciplinary area team under Children's Services. They form an important resource for a school, especially when they work there on a regular basis. Their role is often linked to providing advice for Statements or, in future, EHC plans. The Educational Psychologist (EP) can be invaluable when giving advice to teachers about pupil behaviour or pupils causing concern. EPs often run projects to develop new strategies or techniques and support staff development. Schools may want to purchase additional EP support, either from the local service or another provider.

Learning support services

These vary greatly across LAs in both availability and composition. A typical team might consist of a number of teacher specialists in a range of disabilities, such as autism; speech, language and communication; moderate learning difficulties; severe learning difficulties; and dyslexia. Teachers of the deaf and visually impaired (who must have mandatory qualifications) are sometimes attached to such a team, or may work on the basis of outreach from a special school where this is nearby. There are statutory requirements for teachers of the deaf and visually impaired, in that they are required to give assessment advice to children with such disabilities. These support teams work in an advisory capacity, or help SENCos with assessment and planning. Some LAs run these services; in others, schools buy what they require through service-level agreements between the school and the service, which may be privately owned. The SENCo's role is evolving toward being a commissioner of services, a negotiator working with a range of support services to ensure the provision appropriate to children and young people's specific needs and a manager of those carrying out the support within the school. The Quality Standards for SEN support and outreach services (DCSF 2008d) offer useful guidance to schools when deciding on service providers.

Education Welfare Officers (EWOs)

EWOs are employed to help parents/carers, as well as to help LAs meet statutory regulations in relation to school attendance. They could play an important role with pupils who also have SEN, in helping to liaise between home and school and maintaining communication in cases where attendance is sporadic. There are often underlying reasons for poor attendance which relate to learning or behavioural difficulties. EWOs could provide support and counselling for those children not in school or at risk of exclusion. This service no longer exists universally. Mansell (2014) reports that due to squeezed budgets and spreading Academy status, particularly among secondary schools, this service has been changed or cut in many places. Some LAs have a service running out of a special school or their Pupil Referral Unit (PRU), which may also cover aspects of non-attendance or potential exclusion. Some Academies have a Home Liaison Officer, but this cannot replace all of the roles played by the LA's EWO. For example, a single school will not carry out truancy sweeps across the local district.

Pupil Referral Units (PRUs)

These units were set up under the 1996 Education Act to offer local provision for pupils who were out of school, usually through exclusion. Many such pupils have social or emotional needs; some will have Statements or, in future, EHC plans. Some PRUs have an outreach service consisting of a team focused on pupils whose attendance and/or behaviour is causing a problem. Personnel are likely to include an EP, behaviour support staff and social workers, although others from the health service may also be included.

Parent Partnership Services (PPS)

This is a national network with representation in each LA and gives free confidential advice, information and support to parents and carers. The service is statutory, but is expected to work at 'arm's length' from the LA. Its purpose is to provide unbiased information and support to parents/carers, often in relation to the statutory assessment procedures, but also about other aspects of education such as exclusions. LAs have a responsibility to provide mediation services or give access to these. Some may come from voluntary organisations, such as the charity KIDs (see *Source List – Organisations*).

Parent/carer forums

These are established in most areas, and are representative local groups of parents/carers of children and young people with disabilities who work alongside the LA and health and social care providers to monitor those services, ensuring they meet the needs of children and families.

Child health services

Many District Health Authorities do not overlap geographically with LAs. There may therefore be more than one health authority with which an LA must communicate. The SENCo needs to know which is the relevant authority for their school. A school's first point of contact will be the local school health service, often the school nurse. Speech and language therapists, occupational therapists and physiotherapists and community paediatricians may work with schools. Local hospitals will also have a paediatric service in which physiotherapists and occupational therapists work. Just how much hospital services can work with schools varies enormously from district to district. Schools may consult health services, with the parent/carer's consent, when wishing to check whether there is a medical condition which may be contributing to a child's difficulty in school.

If necessary, and with informed consent and involvement of the child's parents/carers, a special medical examination can be requested. It is wise to check that hearing and vision, for example, have been examined. The school health service will have records of school-aged children, especially if there are known special needs, which can be accessed as necessary.

Pupils on regular medication for conditions such as asthma, diabetes or epilepsy do not have special educational needs as such, but may miss some schooling. Certain pupils may have aids and appliances which need to be maintained by a clinical technician – hearing aids are an obvious example. Children with more severe disabilities will have been identified in early childhood by the Health Authority and the LA will have been notified. Chapter 3 of the SEND Code of Practice (DfE/DoH 2015) describes in some detail the joint commissioning duties between education and health services.

Child and Adolescent Mental Health Services (CAMHS)

Some children and young people identified as having SEN may benefit from referral to CAMHS – specialists in assessment and interventions for mental health problems. Referrals can come from GPs, schools or other relevant professionals. CAMHS can also provide support and consultation to family members, carers and relevant workers from health, social care, educational and voluntary agencies. Permission from parents and carers must be sought to enable CAMHS to share information with schools. This service is funded by Clinical Commissioning Groups, LAs and the NHS, but the level of funding varies across the country. The charity 'Young Minds' has reported budget cuts to CAMHS services at both NHS and LA levels. Murray (2014) reports that head teachers experience long waiting times for these services, resulting in delays in getting the necessary diagnosis and support for very distressed and vulnerable children and their families. CAMHS should be working collaboratively, but when resources are stretched this becomes a challenge.

Social services

Social service departments should ensure that all schools in their area know the name of and how to contact the designated social services officer with responsibility for 'looked-after' children. Every child who is 'looked after' by the local authority must have a care plan which sets out their long term objectives. Not all such children will have SEN, and so some may not be the responsibility of the SENCo. Liaison within school between SEN and pastoral systems will be important in these cases. The SEN policy needs to set out clearly the arrangements for working in partnership with social services, and who on the school staff has responsibility for 'looked-after' children.

The LO should list child care provision and leisure activities, as well as information for parents/carers about short breaks and details of support groups for those with disabled children. The LA should list services for young people to help them make the transition into adulthood and working life. The Connexions service is no longer universal, but the LO should make clear what arrangements are in place. Personal advisers will be required to link to specialist services or help with college choices. The service should give greater priority to those young people at greatest risk (see also *Chapter 8*).

Voluntary organisations

Over decades a range of disability groups have set up charities to help parents, children and young people, and, in some cases, to run special schools and train specialist teachers. Many of these are long-established and well known – for instance the RNIB, RNID, SCOPE, ICAN and NAS. All are involved in providing training and consultancy services. There are large numbers of smaller groups specialising in a wide range of disabilities (see *Source List*). Other voluntary organisations have more general aims, such as the Council for Disabled Children, which is 'an umbrella body for disabled children in England with links to other UK nations [that] aims to maximize influence on national policies and promote inclusive practice' (www.councilfordisabledchildren. org.uk). The Council for Disabled Children also supports a national group of disabled young people called EPIC (standing for Equality, Partnership, Influence and Change) who were set up to advise the government on changes to the Children & Families Bill. One of the key roles of voluntary organisations is to put parents/carers in touch with others in the same situation as themselves. This, combined with factual information about the disability, is one of the most important ways in which voluntary organisations can be used.

The SENCo's role in working within the multi-professional network

The SEND Code of Practice (DfE/DoH 2015) explains:

> Schools may involve specialists at any point to advise them on early identification of SEN and effective support and interventions. The pupil's parents should always be involved in any decision to involve specialists. The involvement of specialists and what was discussed or agreed should be recorded and shared with the parents and teaching staff supporting the child in the same way as other SEN support.
>
> (DfE/DoH 2015: 6.59)

Both the SEND Regulations (2014) and the NASENCO outcomes emphasise the role of the SENCo in liaising with, and being a key point of contact for, external agencies as sources of support and expertise. This may include the interpretation of specialist assessment data and its use to inform practice. The SENCo's role is evolving toward that of a consumer of services, a negotiator, working with a range of support services to provide appropriately for children and young people. Therefore SENCos should be aware of provision in the LO and be able to work with professionals from beyond the school. The Code (2015: 6.91) (DfE/DoH 2015) recommends that SENCos are provided with sufficient administrative support to allow them to fulfil their duties. This includes easy access to a telephone.

The SENCo often plays a co-coordinating role for parents/carers by putting them in touch with the multi-professional network, or by collating information from the various agencies who may work with the child and family. All parents/carers have a key role to play in their children's care, especially those with SEN. But parents/carers vary, from 'key workers' who have for years co-ordinated information about their child to those who lack confidence and need encouragement to share information and make decisions with the school. The

SENCo also has a role in leading other staff and ensuring that continuing professional development (CPD) opportunities are appropriate with regard to the various aspects of SEN, including working in partnership with those beyond the school.

In very complex cases the child may be known to up to 30 professionals. In such complex disability cases the parent may, in reality, be the key worker for their child, linking the therapies and advice together into an individual plan. Notes will be kept by each service in their files, but it is the parent who has the total picture. In cases where, for example, therapists require programmes of practice at home, there may not be much time for school homework as well. The overarching purpose for support should be to support the teacher or parent to support the child. School support services cannot focus on the parent's own needs, but they can support parents/carers to support their children.

A SENCo may be required to attend multi-agency meetings. This, like any other partnership, has resource implications (for example, the need for supply cover). For multi-agency meetings to be effective, good planning, leadership and good recording are all necessary, to avoid repetition of information-sharing and actions.

Common Assessment Framework (CAF)

As described in *Chapter 1*, the Common Assessment Framework (CAF) was developed as a standardised approach to assessment and decision-making, intended to be a simple holistic process assessing a child's needs and strengths. It was intended for use by all practitioners from education, health and social services in partnership with the family, and aimed to improve integrated working by promoting co-ordinated service provision. Its watchwords are swift and easy access, early identification and prevention and the importance for children's needs to be seen within the context of their families' needs. Children who need the support of several specialist agencies could have a lead professional to co-ordinate services for them. This person will be the single point of contact for families; the SENCo may very well take on this role, or may be the school link. While CAF is not universally used now, there is still a need to co-ordinate services.

SENCos, along with other school staff, will need to collaborate with practitioners such as social workers, nurses, general practitioners, therapists, hospital consultants and educational psychologists; this may involve joint training or working, or encouraging others in services such as housing, young parent or youth offending services to support what the school is doing in specific areas.

Getting to know key workers from health/social services

Because the focus of the work of health or social service personnel is different from that of the school, they will have different priorities. One way to overcome potential professional barriers is to get to know the individual worker on an informal basis outside of the case conference or meeting situation. Inviting professionals to school staff meetings to explain their roles and share ideas with teachers and TAs can be very helpful. Joint working practices can then be decided: then, when there is a problem to be solved, this joint understanding will lead to better results. The school nurse, for example, is a resource that is undervalued in many schools. Therapists and other health and social work professionals may also be persuaded to visit schools on a one-off basis as part of an awareness training session. Referrals to the service may initially be through the regular key worker, but that person will often know someone else who can help in special cases. EPs usually have good contacts with health and social services and may be the first contact for many referrals. On the other hand, some specialist services, e.g. hearing and vision, prefer direct contact.

From the above it is clear that, as part of their SEN policy, schools need to develop their procedures for referrals and requests to support services and agencies, in conjunction with their own LA's Local Offer. Where there are a number of possible choices, decisions need to be made about the best route for support and advice. Over-referral to a number of agencies at one time, for the same case, is ineffective and wasteful of scarce resources. Some schools hold a regular half-termly SEN training meeting in order to prioritise referrals to outside agencies.

Services working collaboratively with teachers and SENCos

Often overwhelming demand from teachers when getting outside advice and support is for strategies to meet the 'Wave 3' intervention targets for SEN support, which are manageable within the normal structure of daily teaching. Some services, therefore – though excellent for carrying out assessment and 'teasing out' any within-child factors causing a problem – may not directly support teachers or SENCos. An understanding of the curriculum and of the social context of the classroom and school is needed if staff are to be fully supported in meeting the needs of more complex individuals. Specialist equipment can help many pupils with SEN, but knowing which equipment or software to buy and whether it will fit the pupils' needs requires expertise. Teachers may need to borrow equipment for a short time to test it for suitability and receive training on its usage. The SENCo should keep track of the extra resources provided or borrowed and be accountable for their efficient use.

Joint problem-solving sessions

There are a number of puzzling pupils for whom it is not quite clear what is needed. Often the way to support these pupils most effectively will be to enhance their teacher's own professional skills in the management of the class. If a visiting professional can find time for a joint problem-solving session with a group of staff, they can together elicit the information already known and produce questions which then can be followed up in an assessment. This will give the staff some strategies to try themselves, as well as providing added focus on the type of further information needed and from whom it could be expected. Such sessions make good use of scarce professional expertise and help teachers realise they may already have answers to some of their questions. This means services must meet teachers' needs as well as the child's. If a teacher feels supported by knowledge that she or he is doing the right thing, and can see the pupil taking a full part in school life and making progress, this will have been a piece of effective support. If, on the other hand, the expert advice has puzzled, confused or de-skilled the teacher, support will not have been so effective.

This chapter has described in some detail the complexity of working within a multi-professional network, and in others beyond the school. SENCos will need to develop their own style of working which fits the context of their school and LA and its Local Offer. Internal school organisation also varies enormously. In some schools, heads and senior managers deal with the outside agencies; in others it is part of the SENCo's role. Whatever the system, communication will be the key issue if the SENCo is to carry out their role effectively.

CHAPTER 8

Working in Partnership at Transition Periods

In the natural process of growing up, children and young people must get used to transition. On a day-to-day basis, many transitions are experienced: moving from home to school or from class to class; entering the playground environment; having a new teacher or teaching assistant; leaving education and entering adulthood. Most pupils take these changes in their stride and are able to adapt well. However, life transitions are often more difficult for some children, depending on the nature of their SEND, and may prove challenging. This needs to be recognised and managed with special care, as the impacts of change can cause anxiety, which in turn reduces curiosity about the world and the ability to learn effectively. This is especially true of children on the autistic spectrum, where routines help, as do visual timetables. The effect of change can be ameliorated with thoughtful planning by staff and discussion with the pupil.

However, there are key points in a child or young person's life when transition between settings requires especial care. Good planning, record-keeping and communication will make a great deal of difference to well-being. Planning for those with a physical disability may involve therapists. There are three critical action times:

- *Entry to school* – planned entry is necessary for children identified in pre-school as having special educational needs or a disability, with or without an EHC plan;
- *Transition between phases or schools* – usually primary to secondary, although infant to junior or first to middle are possible, as are changes due to moving house;
- *Leaving school* – for college, training or adult life. This involves a transition plan for pupils with Statements or EHC plans, but there should be a plan for all pupils with identified SEND.

All of these may involve working in a multi-disciplinary partnership. School policies should include a section where transfer procedures and the roles and responsibilities related to flow of information are made clear. The SENCo needs to take a strong lead in helping colleagues to plan both entry and departure from the school for pupils with SEN.

Early years and entry to school

Certain children have their special needs identified shortly after birth, or before they are two or three years old. Health professionals will often have taken the lead in this identification process and will have informed the LA, who may carry out multi-professional assessments for an EHC plan for those whose needs warrant this. Education offers some pre-school services – for example, a Portage home visiting service, which works directly with parents using a developmental checklist to identify the next learning step. Services for hearing and vision also make home visits as soon as the disability is identified. Information about all local provision and services for parents and children will be available in the Local Offer (see *Chapter 7*).

Area SENCos

In paragraphs 5.55–5.58, the SEND Code of Practice (DfE/DoH 2015) supports the idea of an area SENCo to work in non-maintained Early Years settings, ideally in a ratio of 1:20. Area SENCos:

- offer support and advice regarding individual children with additional needs within the Early Years Foundation Stage;
- deliver training to Early Years providers;
- support transition planning from home to pre-school and then to school;
- inform parents of impartial local information and services;
- establish effective working links to a range of agencies.

Many LAs also have an under-fives multi-disciplinary panel or team which can give advice about a child's needs to the receiving school. There are important issues regarding entry to school for these more vulnerable children. Arrangements need to be flexible and an offer of gradual entry into the full-time experience of school life should be available. Parents have a vital role to play in this planned entry (see *Chapter 7*).

Transition from nursery to school

The EYFS profile, completed for all children in the final term before they turn five, will provide vital information on those who have received SEN support in the Early Years setting. EHC and SEN Support Reviews should include planning and preparation for transition to another setting or school.

The Code says that 'To support transition, information should be shared by the current setting with the receiving setting. The current setting should agree with parents the information to be shared as part of the planning process' (DfE/DoH 2015: 5.47).

Planning entry to school requires good liaison skills from all concerned. Usually some joint planning will have taken place with the school SENCo or class teacher, using knowledge gained by the personnel who will have worked with the child and family before school entry. Early Years providers must provide to LAs information about assessments they have carried out. For those children who attend more than one setting, providers must take account of all available records or discussions with parents/carers from previous settings.

Disability Rights Commission Code of Practice (2002)

The DRC Code of Practice (2002) explains the duties of the responsible body (governors in the case of maintained schools). This Code gives examples of what can be considered as reasonable adjustments. As the duties are anticipatory, the implication is that admission policies themselves must not be discriminatory. Staff training may also be seen as part of this anticipatory duty.

Moves to a new Local Authority

If a child moves to a new LA, responsibility for the EHC plan will be transferred to that LA from the old one, who must pass on all necessary information, usually on the day of the move. The SEND Code of Practice (DfE/DoH 2015) describes these responsibilities in detail in paragraphs 9.157–9.162, and paragraphs 9.163–9.165 describe the responsibilities of the Clinical Commissioning Group when moves are made. The new LA may bring forward the date of the review or make a new assessment.

Transition from class to class	Internal transfer between classes or between infant and junior departments is also important. For the child, having friends matters, so attention should be paid to friendship groups as well as academic information. Most schools have a new-class visit day in the summer term, so that all children will have met their new teacher and have knowledge of where they are going at the start of the autumn term. Children who move home a great deal are the most vulnerable when it comes to transition planning. Schools with mobile populations work on effective procedures for induction, assessment and contact with the previous school, but each school should have clear policies about newcomers who may arrive without records. It is important that all who teach the child are informed of the child's additional needs. Schools must review the child's progress during the course of the year using normal curriculum and SEN support reviews. Parents should be told by the previous school that records will be passed onto the new school.
Transfer to secondary school	The learning environment in secondary schools is different from that in primary settings, in many ways. For example, in primary school most lessons are taught by the class teacher, and the child has a much clearer idea of what is expected. In secondary school the pupil is taught by many different teachers, who may not be as familiar with the child's special educational needs. There is more movement around the school, which may put a pupil with some SEN at a disadvantage, possibly through mobility difficulties or due to confusion in getting

to lessons on time, and because they will have to carry and organise their equipment. Therefore, planning for pupils transferring to secondary schools must be very carefully executed. For example, making a book/folder with photographs of the school and key members of staff, to be looked at over the summer holiday, helps the child to remember where they might go and who they will work with. Visits should be made to acclimatise the pupil to the new building and meet some of the teachers, especially the SENCo. All records, including SEN records, should be up to date and transferred early enough in the summer term so that those who need to know about the pupil's individual needs have the necessary information.

The school organising the departure needs to make every effort to contact the new school. A planning meeting at an annual review for a pupil with a Statement or EHC plan should include parents and, if possible, someone from the new school. Support services may have a vital role in transition by helping the new school make plans. The receiving school must read all records in good time so that plans are in place before entry, especially for the more vulnerable pupils. This is usually done well for those with sensory or physical disabilities: health personnel typically plan what equipment is needed and discuss mobility issues. Planning for other pupils may be weaker. Yet for all pupils, poor preparation may result in setbacks to learning or, in extreme cases, such a traumatic start to the new school that the pupil never settles. In some secondary schools members of the learning support department visit all tutor groups in the first two weeks of the new school year, in order to meet pupils with SEND and to draw up a 'pen picture' or a 'pupil passport' of those learning characteristics which all staff need to know. Care should be taken to note individual preferences and abilities, but expectations should not be lowered merely because the student appears on the SEN register.

Transition plans at 13+ The SEND Code of Practice (DfE/DoH 2015: 8.9–8.16) explains that Local Authorities **must** ensure that the EHC Plan Review at Year 9, and every review thereafter, includes a focus on preparing for adulthood. Planning **must** be centred on the individual, and **must** explore the child or young person's aspirations and abilities, what they want to be able to do when they leave post-16 education or training and the support they need to achieve their ambitions. Transition planning **must** be built into the revised EHC plan, and should result in clear outcomes being agreed that are ambitious and stretching and which will prepare the young person for adulthood. Chapter 8 of the Code describes transition plan meetings, which are usually held as part of the regular annual review meetings organised by the school and gives details of what transition planning should include. The emphasis is on preparation for adulthood, which continues in each subsequent review. It is the LA's responsibility to ensure that relevant services co-operate in helping to achieve the young person's aspirations. These services will be detailed in the Local Offer (see *Chapter 7*).

Person-centred approach

This was discussed in *Chapter 6*, and the principles here will apply to Transition Reviews. The Children and Families Act (2014), as referred to in the first chapter of the SEND Code of Practice, says that LAs must:

- have regard to the views, wishes and feelings of the child or young person, and the child's parents;
- help them to participate as fully as possible in decisions which help them achieve the best possible educational and other outcomes, preparing them effectively for adulthood.

Bennett (2014) gives useful advice on 'personalising your approach'. The team around the young person must listen to what the young person wants, and include them in the decision-making process.

For decision-making to be effective, there must be access to accurate, up-to-date information, from the Local Offer in particular, as to what services and support are available across education, health and social care.

The plan which is developed at the Transition Review should clarify the young person's 'views, wishes and feelings', and decide on agreed outcomes which will be written into the EHC plan. Additional resources need to be identified and allocated, including personal budgets (see *Chapter 9*).

As Bennett (2014: 43) notes, key principles of the person-centred approach will include:

- focus on the child or young person, not their diagnostic label;
- using ordinary language and images rather than professional jargon;
- actively highlighting a child or young person's strengths;
- enabling the child or young person, and those who know them best, to express their interests and aspirations for the future;
- tailoring support and personal budgets.

The challenge of the transition plan lies in the development of continuity of assessment, review and programme planning from school through further educational, vocational and personal preparation for a valued and productive adult life. The Code makes it very clear that the young person must be actively involved in the development of the transition plan and their views must be taken into account. Gascoigne suggests that parents may find this period very stressful as their feelings will be ambivalent: 'On the one hand they want their child to become as independent as possible, and on the other, they wish to extend their protection of them' (Gascoigne 1995: 38). He emphasises how sensitive parents can be and how much support they will need from those working with them.

Transition plans start in Year 9 and continue annually until the young person leaves school. It is important that all professionals involved build good relationships with the young person and their families and provide to them all information about what is available in their local area. This process is usually carried out very thoroughly in special schools, but should also be available to pupils with SEN in mainstream schools.

Looked-after children

Children in care (looked-after children) may have SEND, and some will have EHC plans. Schools and Academies must appoint a designated teacher for looked-after children and the SENCo must work closely with that teacher. Looked-after children will have a Care Plan which should be taken into account in SEN assessment. Annual reviews of EHC plans should coincide with review of the Care Plan. When transferring to college at 16/17 these children will cease to be 'looked after', but the LA has the responsibility to prepare a pathway plan and provide a personal adviser. If the young person continues in education and training, their EHC plan should ensure good advance planning involving the young person and their adviser.

Transition to post-16 education and training

A key transition point will be leaving school to go to college. The choice of a suitable college will need early preparation and the collection of information to help the young person make their choice. Visits from college staff to the existing school, or visits to colleges, may well be part of this information-gathering process. The young person may need an advocate to help in this process. This could be a member of the school staff who knows the young person well, or alternatively an independent skilled adviser may be appointed to listen to the young person's views. Those with EHC plans may need tailored post-16 pathways. The adviser should be familiar with a range of college provision, and if possible visits should be undertaken with the young person, either with a parent or adviser. The adviser must listen carefully so as to understand the young person's views, feelings and aspirations at all stages. The provision at college must fit the young person's interests – for example sport or performing arts. It would be wrong to push them into areas that do not fit their interests and abilities.

The SEND Code of Practice (DfE/DoH 2015: 7.3) says that all colleges (further education, sixth form, 16–19 Academies and independent specialist colleges) have statutory duties to:

- co-operate with the LA to make arrangements for young people with SEN;
- admit a young person if the institution is specified in their EHC plan;
- use their best endeavours to put appropriate support in place;
- have regard to the Code of Practice.

Additionally, they have duties under the Equality Act (2010) not to discriminate against young people with SEN and to make 'reasonable adjustments' which are anticipatory, meaning that they should be in place before the young person enters the college. It may be helpful to invite a college tutor to the final school review to discuss the support available at the college. Support must be in place at the beginning of the course, as the first few weeks are crucial in terms of student retention. Supported wheelchair access and supported physical care facilities may be required. The Code explains that all students aged 16–19, and those aged up to 25 if they have EHC plans, should follow a coherent study programme which provides stretch and progression.

Colleges would benefit, when planning provision, from year-on-year projections of those with specific types of disabilities. A high level of support in FE may be needed for students with EHC plans or Statements, so it is important that secondary schools communicate information early regarding all vulnerable students who might need support. Colleges should be approached with a view to including entry criteria for all courses in their prospectuses. Admission to courses would then be based on fair and transparent procedures, and not on assumptions or subjective impressions.

Sometimes young people do not want attention to be drawn to their differences by having individual support, and their permission must be sought before information is shared with staff. Transition planning using the local services will be key to the effective planning of further education provision. However, it is vital that the information gathered reaches all who are involved in the enrolment of students.

Planning for entry to college should consider all aspects of the process, including transport to the college. The Local Offer must include information about transport provision. This requirement applies to those up to age 25 with EHC plans. The support provided by the college should be reviewed regularly and, when the young person has an EHC plan, at least annually. The LA has a statutory duty to review, and the college **must** co-operate in the process. The SEND Code of Practice (DfE/DoH 2015: 7.22) strongly advises that 'a named person' be appointed to have oversight of SEN provision, in a similar way to the SENCo's role in schools. In order to help young people and their parents/carers, as well as school SENCos, support staff and other key personnel, it may be helpful to compile a handbook which will include simple, straightforward information about applying for college courses offered, and other practical considerations such as claiming Disability Living Allowance.

The Code of Practice (DfE/DoH 2015) says that transition planning is to continue for those with EHC plans and will continue to focus on preparation for adulthood. Transition to adulthood means gaining independence, knowing how/where to get help, developing life skills, social skills and friendship making. However, it is a sad fact that fewer pupils with SEN continue in education than those without SEN and many are not in education, employment or training post-16. Those who continue in education are more likely to go to a FE college than stay in the school sixth form (DfE Statistical Release, 2014e). The SEND Code of Practice (DfE/DoH 2015) extends its remit to young people up to the age of 25 when they have EHC plans. Some young people will need to transfer to Adult Social Care services at 25.

The Connexions service, or a similar local service, may be used as a bridge from school or college to work placements and apprenticeships.

This can help reassure both student and parent, to ease the transition. The Code emphasises that continuity of provision is essential and that early planning is necessary. An aspiration of the 2014 Children and Families Act is to give young people with SEND greater educational choice, which could mean attending a specialist college away from the local area. This could provide excellent opportunities for the young person to build independence and develop life skills. However, changes in funding arrangements for school leavers with high levels of need may compromise this choice, despite the fact that equipping young people to live semi-independent lives could reduce long-term costs.

Reviewing policy

Transition is part of growing up for all children and young people with SEND and will require planning and support, particularly at the key points described in this chapter. Schools also have the responsibility to prepare all children and young people for adulthood from very early on. Secondary and FE colleges offer Personal, Social & Health Education (PSHE) and Citizenship lessons which, in part, are meant to assist in preparing for adulthood. As with all aspects of support, this should be part of the school or college's policy and its effectiveness should be reviewed regularly. In line with the spirit of the Code, the views of children and young people should be taken into account and acted on so the transition experiences improve.

CHAPTER 9

The SENCo's Role in Leading and Managing SEND Provision

This chapter links with *Chapter 3* on identification, assessment and planning, and continues to describe the SENCo's role in relation to the paperwork and procedures required by the SEND Code of Practice (DfE/DoH 2015). The SENCo shares responsibility for tracking pupils' progress with class teachers and form tutors, and takes a lead role in organising annual reviews for those with EHC plans. This makes demands on the SENCo's time and their management abilities. The chapter also describes special situations in which SENCos are likely to help prepare evidence: a) SEND tribunals and b) Ofsted inspections.

All of the above should be reflected in how roles and responsibilities are allocated and evaluated as part of the school's SEN policy, as described in *Chapter 2*. The work described here is perceived as an important part of the SEN co-ordination, not necessarily to be carried out by the SENCo alone. The head and governors have the ultimate responsibility to see that these tasks are carried out effectively. All of the above will require organisational skills and clarity of purpose and call on interpersonal skills when working in partnership with the child, parent, teachers, senior leaders and other professionals.

Working with governors

As governors have a number of legal duties regarding SEN, most schools have a governor or a committee with responsibility for provision for children and young people. SEND governors need a high degree of awareness of SEN and disability legislation and an understanding of how this applies in practice. As the SENCo is an invaluable source of information, establishing a relationship between governors and the SENCo is important. Regular meetings should be scheduled to brief governors on salient issues and to update them on changing patterns of need within the school and the best provision to make.

Ideally, the SENCo and governing body will work together within a whole-school strategy towards the inclusion and success of children and young people with SEN in all aspects of school life. The SENCo, as a manager, may have an important role in advising governors on the best ways to consult adults and children with SEN in the school community, in line with the Equality Act (2010) (see *Chapter 2*).

The SENCo should see SEN issues in relation to other aspects of equality and help governors to understand the links and make coherent decisions.

As governors also agree the school budget and staffing decisions, the shrewd SENCo will be explicit about the costs of resources, including teaching assistants, hardware and software, and about modifications which may be necessary to buildings and equipment, while ensuring that there is a convincing and evidence-based rationale for any new proposal. Governors must evaluate the impact of any provision that is made and it may be incumbent on the SENCo to supply appropriate data and qualitative information. A provision map will be useful in this.

Provision management

This is a powerful strategic tool to help schools monitor how inclusive their provision is, the progress pupils are making and the effectiveness of SEN resources that are *additional to* and *different from* the highly differentiated curriculum. Provision management is an 'at a glance' way to show all the provision a school makes, as well as to identify pupil needs and the staff skills required to meet them. Deployment of staff can be targeted to closely meet needs identified for both individuals and groups of pupils. Costs can be calculated to enable schools to track their SEN spending. This complete picture or map allows schools to see the impact of their SEN resource provision and identify gaps in provision, and, when linked with assessment, can demonstrate the progress made by pupils over time. Provision management is an excellent way to demonstrate to Ofsted and others precisely what a school is doing to meet SEND needs and how these are contributing to pupil outcomes. The process of provision management and mapping is the responsibility of the whole school, not just the SENCo (see *Source List*).

The management of SEN records

The SEN list/register

This is a list or register of all pupils receiving SEN support in the form of additional resources, including those with EHC plans. The SENCo compiles the list in collaboration with class and subject teachers, who will alert them to any concerns about pupils. This list can be a valuable tool to keep track of pupils both from an SEN viewpoint and in terms of their wider outcomes. By recording the type of need, the SEN resources allocated and progress against these, alongside other relevant factors such as receipt of Pupil Premium or free school meals, ethnicity and EAL, the list feeds into the provision management process and provides strategic information for whole-school planning. With this information kept together in a single place, the 'list' becomes an organic tool that tracks everything necessary about SEN pupils.

SEN records

With class teachers becoming more responsible for meeting the needs of all children through the delivery of a highly differentiated curriculum,

SEN record-keeping will be closely integrated into classroom planning and other whole-school assessment procedures. Progress against learning intentions recorded in teachers' planning provides good evidence for future decision-making about whether a child has SEN or not, as well as further evidence of the need to increase provision where necessary.

SEN support

Where children are in receipt of additional support, a record must be kept of the additional resources provided and progress made as a result of these. For pupils who have significant medical, SEMH and educational needs but do not have an EHC plan, it makes sense to create a single person-centred plan (PCP). This approach amalgamates all previous plans into one cohesive document, including information that was previously written in IEPs.

Where a PCP is used, it must be envisaged as a process as well as a set of documents. Writing one beautiful plan will not suffice; it is the setting of outcomes and evaluating progress against them over time that makes a PCP valuable to pupils, teachers and parents. The PCP will be outcome-focused and take account of the views of the child and the parent. An outcome is defined as 'the benefit or difference made to an individual as a result of an intervention' (DfE/DoH 2015: 9.66).

Organisation of reviews for those receiving SEN support

The whole strength of the graduated approach depends on tracking progress in a regular, thorough manner. As progress tracking is now required for all pupils, it is up to schools to develop methods that work for teachers and pupils while still complying with the main principles of the Code (2014). These must identify and meet the needs of all pupils and give every child full access to the curriculum and life of the school. In classes where there are groups of children with similar needs, these can be met through teachers' regular planning; therefore, personal plans will not be necessary.

Running reviews is very time-consuming for the class or subject teacher as well as for the SENCo. As parent and pupil views are to be fully incorporated, this too makes enormous demands on a school's resource of time. Therefore, careful thought should be given when deciding who needs a personal plan. When possible, reviews should take place with the regular cycles of parents' evenings. It is possible to be very creative about these meetings – with parental agreement, they may take place via other media such as Skype or phone. Training is essential for staff involved in review meetings, as they require a considerable amount of skill. Specialists from beyond the school will often be involved. Sometimes the cycle of reviews will show that the child's needs are not being met within the school's present resources and further assessment may be required, at which point a request for an EHC assessment may be made.

Referral for an EHC assessment

Very few pupils (1–2 per cent of the population) will have such severe and persistent difficulties that they cannot cope within mainstream education without significant additional or alternative provision. If the school has carried out all the work of graduated assessment and review and, after consultation with the support services and the parents, they all agree, then a request for an EHC assessment can be made by a suitable member of the school staff, such as the headteacher or SENCo, to the LA. Parents can also request an EHC assessment, as can a young person over the age of 16 and under 25. Other relevant professionals/carers can also request an EHC assessment (see DfE/DoH 2015: 9.8).

An EHC assessment should not normally be a first step, but should follow on from planning already undertaken (see DfE/DoH 2015: 9.3). The Local Authority will then request evidence from the school or provider about the provision already in place and the progress made. The LA will look for evidence that 'despite the provider having taken relevant and purposeful action, the child or young person has not made expected progress' (DfE/DoH 2015: 9.14).

The LA must notify the parent or young person that it is considering whether an EHC assessment is necessary. The parent or young person must have time to provide their views, and must be supported in the decision-making process (see DfE/DoH 2015: 9.12). All those requested to provide advice for the EHC assessment must do this within six weeks (see *Appendix 9*). Schools will be asked to collect and collate all relevant documentation, including information from their records about progress. An EHC assessment is not always carried out following a request. If the LA decides not to make an EHC assessment, they must inform the child's parents or young person within 16 weeks, as well as informing them of their right to appeal and their right to mediation if necessary.

The EHC plan

Once the EHC assessment has taken place, as is explained in Chapter 9 of the SEND Code of Practice (DfE/DoH 2015), LAs should prepare a draft EHC plan. It is very important for the LA to consider how best to achieve the outcomes sought by the child/young person. These will include education, training, health and care outcomes, as well as such considerations as positive social relationships (DfE/DoH 2015: 9.64).

The draft plan, with all its appendices (see *Appendix 9*), must be sent to the parent or young person, and at least 15 days must be allowed for them to consider it and make comments. The draft plan *must not* contain the name of the nursery, school or college to be attended, but parents must be given access to information to aid their choice (DfE/DoH 2015: 9.77).

Paragraphs 9.78–9.94 of the Code explain the procedures for choice of institutions and consultation with the one that is chosen by the parent or young person, including a description of what are called 'reasonable steps' that could be taken by mainstream institutions.

Once the draft is amended and agreed, the LA issues a final plan. Where a nursery, school or college is named in this final plan, they must admit the child/young person and put appropriate provision in place to meet their needs.

Annual Reviews for those with EHC plans

The full details of annual review procedures are published in Chapter 9 of the SEND Code of Practice (DfE/DoH 2015: 9.166–9.176). Reviews for those leaving school are an important part of transition planning (see *Chapter 8*). LAs have a duty to review all Statements and EHC plans at least annually. The Code says that the review meeting must focus on the child or young person's progress towards achieving the outcomes specified in the EHC plan, and on what changes might need to be made to the support that is provided to help them achieve those outcomes, or whether changes are needed to the outcomes themselves. Children, parents and young people should be supported to engage fully in the review meeting.

The first annual review must be held within 12 months of issuing the EHC plan. LAs should provide the headteacher or principal of the school/college with a list of children/young people who will require an annual review of their EHC plan (or Statement) at least two weeks before the start of each term. Reviews are usually held at and by the school, as they know the child best and have the clearest view about progress and the next steps that are required. NASEN advises that schools and their SENCos will need to be 'geared up' to review existing Statements. LAs have three years to convert these to EHC plans. This could involve training at schools, or special arrangements in which LAs hold transition reviews for this process.

Preparation of paperwork

Advance planning is essential, as it takes time to collect reports for an annual review. At least two months in advance of the meeting, the headteacher must request written advice from:

- the child/young person;
- the child's parents/carers;
- those the LA has specified;
- those the headteacher considers appropriate.

These are likely to be the class and support teacher or assistant, any specialist teacher giving advice, an educational psychologist and/or any health and social service professionals involved with the child. Parents may need support with submitting their advice and may welcome a pre-review meeting, especially if this is the first annual review after the Statement was made, or if it is taking place at a transition time when their child is due to change school. An informal meeting may prepare the parent for the more formal review meeting. Parents can find annual reviews stressful, so a preparation meeting can provide an opportunity to answer their questions and ensure they feel confident that their views have been noted.

The review meeting

Person Centred Planning is a way of empowering people to plan their future and organise services they need. Some LAs and schools are beginning to incorporate these ideas into the annual review process. The aim is to support the pupil and parents through preparation in the way the review is conducted. For example, these points should be covered:

- how the room is set out to put the child and parent/carer at ease;
- respecting the child's and parents'/carers' preferred means of communication;
- inviting those present to record their view of the child's strengths and progress on flip-charts round the room; start with positives, about what we like and admire;
- consider a range of issues such as what is working/not working; what is important to the child and important to their health and support needs;
- acknowledge that people have different perspectives, but draw these together into a time-limited action plan showing what each person involved should aim to achieve;
- record questions that remain unanswered.

After the review

- Within two weeks of the Review Meeting, the school must prepare a report which summarises the outcomes of this meeting. The report is then circulated to all those who were invited to the meeting, and must be sent to the LA.
- The report will set out recommendations for any amendments required to the EHC plan (or Statement). It sets interim targets for the coming year and, if appropriate, new outcomes that have been agreed. It is important that the child's/young person's and the parents' views, wishes and feelings are recorded.
- Within four weeks, the LA must decide whether or not to amend the EHC plan or to cease to maintain it, and then notify the parents/young person and the school of these decisions.

Dealing with complaints

The SEN Regulations (2014) (see *Appendix 2a*) state that schools must publish 'Any arrangements made by the governing body or the proprietor relating to the treatment of complaints from parents of pupils with special educational needs concerning the provision made at the school'. Schools usually have a general complaints system, but particular attention must be given to SEN complaints. Often it is the class teacher or the SENCo to whom the parent first turns. This is the best action if the matter can be dealt with easily. It should be kept clearly in mind that the headteacher has the final responsibility for the school, along with the governors. It is important therefore that procedures are clearly set out and published, and not left to chance. If schools make sure parents are fully informed throughout the assessment procedures and are given access to the LA Parent Partnership Scheme as early as possible, it should be possible to allay fears and avoid complaints. Ultimately, parents may have recourse to the First-Tier Tribunal (SEN and Disability) if they are not satisfied with the school's actions. It is wise therefore to have an agreed policy not only for ordinary complaints to the school, but also for cases where the parent may appeal against an LA decision – whether this is a decision not to assess or reassess a child, a decision not to issue an EHC plan or a decision about the contents of the plan.

Mediation services

The CoP (DfE/DoH 2015) sections 11.4–11.5 describe the role of mediation services which must be offered to parents/young people before an appeal to the Tribunal is made. LAs have a duty to make arrangements for an independent mediation service whose advisers have received relevant training. These arrangements should be set out in the Local Offer (see *Chapter 7*). The idea is that, if at all possible, the mediation will be able to clarify the nature of the parent's/young person's disagreement with the LA and settle this, without the need for an appeal to the Tribunal, in an 'informal, non-legalistic, accessible and simple' way. However, once contact with the mediation adviser has been made, should the parent/young person decide not to go to mediation, the adviser will issue a certificate; without this, registration of an appeal cannot be made.

The SEND Tribunal

This tribunal is part of the First-Tier Tribunal (Health, Education and Social Care Chamber), overseen by Her Majesty's Courts & Tribunal Service. The SEND Tribunal hears appeals against decisions made by LAs in relation to EHC assessments and plans. It also hears disability discrimination claims against schools. Appeals are heard by a judge and panel of tribunal members with experience of SEN or disability. Hearings take place throughout the country, as close to the parents' home as possible. Parents and young people can appeal with regard to specified elements of their EHC assessment or plan, such as:

• the description of the child/young person;
• the type of provision described;
• the type of school or institution, or the fact that no school has been specified.

They can also appeal against the LA's decision not to assess or to reassess, or when the LA decides to cease to maintain the EHC plan. The Tribunal does not normally hear appeals concerning health and social care elements of the EHC plan, or concerning personal budgets. However, parents and young people *do* have the right to appeal to the Tribunal about provision of health or social care when this is treated as wholly or mainly educational provision. For example, speech therapy is normally seen as fundamental to education, and the LA is ultimately responsible for ensuring that it is provided.

The school's role in tribunal cases

In all tribunal cases, schools will be expected to provide detailed information about the child's/young person's SEN or disability, actions taken by the school and evidence of progress made. The SENCo may be asked to collate this detailed evidence. When well-kept records are available, these should show types of interventions and support given by the school, and possibly the reasons why the specific needs can no longer be met. The views of parents and children/young people will, over time, also be an important part of this evidence.

In some cases, a named representative of the school could be asked by a parent to be a voluntary witness. It is also possible for the Tribunal to issue an order for attendance for a member of the school's staff. Sometimes schools may agree with the parents' appeal to the tribunal against the LA. In other situations schools might agree with the LA. In both cases the school can feel it is caught between the LA and the parent, and so the whole context of the tribunal hearing and its preparation can cause stress for all concerned. Where parents have appealed against an LA decision, there are two very important requirements for the school. First, it must be able to give evidence of how assessments, interventions and progress tracking have been carried out; second, it must show that everything possible has been done to maintain normal professional relationships with the parents. Staff need not agree with everything about the parents' appeal or the LA's response – indeed, the school should at all times focus on its contribution, supported by evidence, of factual information about the educational needs of the child and the provision necessary to ensure success in learning. School staff should be aware throughout the process of appeal that they will have to continue to work closely with the parents after the hearing and that the LA and parents must comply with the Tribunal Order.

Preparation by the SENCo for an Ofsted inspection

When inspecting SEN provision, inspectors will evaluate the progress made by pupils who have SEN without a Statement or EHC plan (pupils receiving SEN support) against the progress of children without SEN. Evidence of how the school is narrowing the gap between these two groups to show that pupils with SEN are making at least the expected rates of progress from their starting point is required. SEN issues permeate the entire inspection framework.

Achievement

Inspectors are looking for clear evidence of how baseline data, including teacher assessment, test results and RAISEonline data, is used to plan and adjust SEN provision. The rate of progress relative to a child's starting point should tell a positive story about the progress of pupils with SEN (see *Chapter 2*). It is important to show evidence of the use of target-setting that challenges pupils and leads to high expectations. Schools need to organise and record evidence from moderation processes, to ensure there is a common understanding of achievement for those performing below age-related expectations.

Where pupils receive provision that is '*additional to and different from*' their peers, inspectors will expect 'accelerated progress' for the majority of the SEN cohort. For a few individual children with very high-level needs, more detailed information, possibly a case study, will be needed. Much of the data gathered will help to show patterns achieved by different groups of pupils, such as looked-after children, those with SEN or EAL, travellers and refugees, as well as progress for individual students.

It is essential that the SENCo can evaluate the school data and demonstrate that effective use of resources is being made. Since it is likely that a high proportion of the SEN cohort will also receive the Pupil Premium, SENCos should be able to show how that additional resource stream is benefiting these pupils.

Quality of teaching

In addition to inspecting the quality of a highly differentiated curriculum, inspectors will be looking for the impact of additional resources on pupils' learning. The largest additional resource is usually the provision of staffing, often teaching assistants. In addition, specialist teachers and programmes such as speech and language therapy are used to enhance provision for pupils with SEND. Devising a way to measure the impact of additional resources is important and sometimes challenging. Improved outcomes in learning are measured using school and national data sets. Judgement on the quality of teaching is primarily concerned with academic achievement, based on a range of evidence, including lesson observation, scrutiny of pupils' work and teacher planning.

Behaviour can often be measured from behaviour and incident logs. These will be included in the wider inspection judgements on the overall effectiveness of the school. A reduction in the number of times a young person's name is entered on the serious incident log can show improvement. Pupils' work is central to the judgement of quality of teaching, so SENCos must be involved in regular work scrutiny.

Behaviour and safety

All staff are responsible for following the Keeping Children Safe in Education (DfE 2014d) requirements. The SENCo must ensure that SEN pupils are not over-represented in negative indicators such as:

• exclusions
• poor attendance
• bullying.

All behaviour management procedures must be underpinned by a behaviour policy. The standards of behaviour and safety of pupils with SEN are expected to be the same as that for other pupils; as such, inspectors will look at exclusion data and the proportion of both fixed-term and permanent exclusions for pupils with SEN and other vulnerable groups in the school. Understanding patterns of poor behaviour and exclusions enables schools to explain and address any anomalies.

Leadership and management

Governors and school leaders must ensure that the needs of the population with SEN are provided for. Inspectors will examine how well pupils with SEN progress both academically and socially from their starting points by examining SEN systems, lesson observations, work scrutiny and discussion with the SEN leader in the school, who is usually the SENCo. Useful documentation to have in place includes:

- an up-to-date provision map, detailing identified needs, provision to meet them and expected outcomes;
- case studies of several pupils illustrating their needs, provision and the progress made as a result of the actions taken by the school;
- evidence of review cycles and planning for pupils with SEND, including IEPs and pupil-centred plans where they exist;
- evidence of an SEN register or list;
- up-to-date SEN policy as part of the SEN information report required on school websites;
- information on the use of formative and summative assessment systems. The Transition Matrices within RAISEonline provide information about the progress of pupils working below age-related expectations;
- evidence that parents and pupils are actively involved in decision-making about SEN.

A folder with examples of data and how it is used, case studies, meeting cycles, review cycles and supporting paperwork will provide the starting point for discussion. It is essential that the SENCo can talk convincingly about how school data informs practice. The SENCo must be able to show that there is no increasing gap between the progress of pupils with and without SEN.

Funding for personal budgets

As was described in *Chapter 2* on SEN funding, there are three elements to a school's budget:

- Universal (per capita funding);
- Targeted Support element, managed by the school;
- High Needs element.

The SEN Code of Practice (2015) (DfE/DoH 2015) explains that personal budgets will be resourced from the High Needs element. Personal budgets could also have contributions from health or social care. A SEN personal budget enables support to be personalised to meet individual needs which cannot be met by mainstream or targeted support. The personal budget is agreed with those drawing up the EHC plan as an indicative budget which is only available when the EHC plan is finalised. The Code (2015: 9.101) explains that there are four ways in which the parent or young person can be involved in securing provision. One of these is for the family to receive direct payments, to contract and manage services themselves. Another is for the LA, or the school/college, to hold funds and commission support, specified in the EHC plan as a 'notional budget'. The concept of personal budgets is new to education, and there will have to be a period during which the processes are developed by schools/colleges and LAs.

Summary

This chapter has described the core of the SENCo's administrative work:

- monitoring of individual and group planning for all pupils with SEN;
- the maintenance of records and organisation of review procedures associated with the Code of Practice;
- data monitoring and preparation of paperwork or information to feed into reviews of the school policy or development plan, or for an Ofsted inspection.

The prime aim of all of these tasks is to improve the opportunities for pupils with SEN to learn effectively, access the curriculum, make progress and be valued as full members of the school community. The SENCo can help make this happen if they can both organise efficiently and work in a supportive way with all concerned.

CHAPTER 10

The SENCo's Role in Leading and Managing Change

The SENCo's role has been developing and changing over the past decades toward one of strategic leadership and management. SENCos training for their role on National Award programmes are often encouraged to experience change management, if only while under-taking projects for their coursework. This chapter will support SENCos in developing a robust knowledge and understanding of the theoretical, practical and political aspects of leading and manag-ing change.

Rationale and principles for change

Change is endemic in education, and the area of special needs is no exception. Change derives from both inside and outside schools. Successive government legislation and strategies have put continual pressure on schools to change policy and practice in relation to SEN and disability (see *Chapter 1*). The SEND Code of Practice (DfE/DoH 2015) is a prime example of an external influence on schools to change, as it revises many SEN procedures and changes focus (see all previous chapters).

Significant changes which the SEND Code of Practice (DfE/DoH 2015) introduces include:

• Developing partnership with parents, children and young people in order for them to take an active part in decision-making (see *Chapters 6* and *8*).
• Multi-agency working between education, health and social care, especially in developing EHC plans to replace Statements; the role of the LA in producing and publishing its Local Offer (see *Chapters 7* and *9*).
• Class and subject teachers are to take full responsibility for the progress of all children, including those with SEN (see *Chapters 3, 4* and *5*).

These changes will affect schools' SEN policy and practice, and adap-tations will be necessary. The rest of this chapter will explore, in some detail, how these changes can be successfully managed.

The SENCo's role, in conjunction with senior leaders, is to decide how to make these changes to current systems and how best to man-age the process so that staff, parents and pupils experience a smooth transition and outcomes for pupils are improved. As was discussed in *Chapter 2*, both time available and status will influence what can be done. SENCos who are part of the senior leadership team and are therefore part of the strategic decision-making in the school can effect whole-school change in relation to SEN, but others can effect small-scale changes. Despite rapid change, effective leadership and management can create excitement and energy. Careful planning and an understanding of the factors that make change effective are pre-requisites to success.

Golden rules for change

Cowne (2003) adapted ideas first expounded by Georgiades and Phil-limore (1975) to develop what she called the four golden rules for SENCos. These are especially relevant if the SENCo starts a change management project alone or a course project with a few colleagues.

The first rule is *small is beautiful*: it is essential to choose an area of policy/practice which is small enough to be the focus of a short project lasting a term or so. This could be a pilot for a longer-term project. The second rule is *go with the flow*: this means choosing something that is part of ongoing school development, or, in the case of implementation of the SEND Code of Practice (DfE/DoH 2015), an area which concerns most staff, preferably building on what is in place. As a start, an audit might be used (see *Activity 1*). The third rule is *do not get eaten for breakfast*: this is advice not to jump into the most difficult aspect, where most staff will be resistant. Schools are like dragons, and will eat up these 'hero innovators'.

The fourth rule follows on from this and is *Work with the healthy parts of the system*: when planning change, choose people who are supportive rather than those whom you perceive require the most change. Your supporters will work with you and be adaptable to modification, whereas dissenters may try to sabotage your efforts.

Emotional response to change

Understanding and using tried-and-tested change management pro-cesses will boost the chances of successful leadership and management of change. Managing change is as much about emotional responses to change as the change process itself. The Change Management Curve (DfE 2001) offers a useful perspective on this (see Figure 10.1).

Staff may experience a range of emotions when going through change in the workplace. They may go through any or all of these stages at any time prior to or during a change process. In recognising this, SENCos can respond appropriately to their colleagues with sup-port and encouragement. It is important to be proactive when change is planned, anticipating possible insecurity and providing reassurance and creating opportunities among colleagues for issues, thoughts and feelings to be discussed.

Change is successful only once it has become fully embedded in the school system. This takes much longer than anticipated. Creat-ing a change management team is an effective way of planning and implementing change. Choose colleagues who will provide different

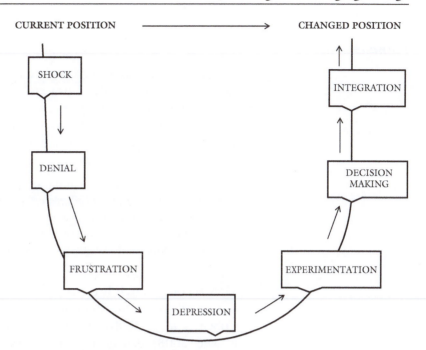

Figure 10.1 Change Management Curve.

Source: Handling Change Toolkit VO1 (DfE 2001).

points of view and who represent the main stakeholder groups that will be affected (see Bolman and Deal 1997, discussed below). Working only with like-minded people may not bring about sustainable and effective change. Engaging the support and encouragement of senior leaders must also be a priority, as they will set aside time and resources and, most importantly, send the message to the school that this is important.

The importance of communication

Communication about change is essential, but it is important to get the balance right. Too much, or too little, or too late will be disruptive and may create cynicism. Be careful about the use of e-mail to communicate change. Emails are useful because they are quick and reach large numbers of people; however, it is difficult to know how individuals will interpret their contents. Keep messages short and factual and always allow opportunities to talk face-to-face so that personal reactions can be assessed. This helps keep track of the 'temperature' of the change process. Publicising frequently asked questions (with answers, of course) is very useful, and communicating on a personal basis wherever possible is desirable. Change takes time and energy, but this is well invested if it is to be successful. Setting up a prominent real or virtual SEN noticeboard and drawing members of staff's attention to the information displayed is an effective way of communication. Remember to keep the information up to date, highlighting any news and offering, for example, 'surgeries' that enable staff to air their own questions and anxieties face-to-face.

Models of change management

Action research

Action research is a form of practitioner research carried out by teachers in their own schools and could be a useful tool for giving structure to the necessary stages and processes of change management. The essence of action research is its cyclical nature. It moves in a potentially unending cycle of decision-making – action taken as a result of investigation or development of policy or practice and reflection on outcomes (see Figure 10.2).

> Action research may be used in almost any setting where a problem involving people, tasks and procedures cries out for solution, or where some change of feature results in a more desirable outcome. To do action research is to plan, act, observe and reflect more carefully, more systematically and more rigorously than one usually does in everyday life.
>
> (Kemmis and McTaggart 1992:26)

Thus action research is concerned with changing individuals or the culture of groups, institutions and societies to which they belong. Cohen *et al.*'s (2000) original eight-stage model, as simplified in Cowne (2003), defines stages in the process as follows:

Problem identification

Here, the decision is made as to where to start, identifying an aspect of policy or practice to be developed and expressed as a research question. An audit such as that shown in *Activity 1* could be used.

Problem illumination

Initial data is collected to build a 'rich picture'. This establishes what is in place already in the chosen area, and what members of

Figure 10.2 Action Research Cycle.

staff's views are about it. A useful tool at this stage is the 'Learning Walk':

> Learning Walks are a very structured method of gathering evidence of progress against a clearly defined issue, and planning ways forward. It is a collaborative activity carried out by a team of people, who together define or refine the issue, and the best way to gather evidence.
>
> (Frankl 2007: see *Source List* for more information)

Evidence is usually gathered from short, focused lesson observations or interviews with relevant staff or pupils.

Action

An action plan is drawn up to trial the innovation or change. This includes a timescale and success criteria. The plan is put into effect. Data is collected about the innovation and its success (see *Appendix 10a*).

Evaluation and reflection

This is an essential part of the action research cycle. The findings are evaluated and discussed, checking that the research question has been addressed. Conclusions are presented to staff and reflection on what has been learnt takes place. At this point, a new question may be formed and the whole process repeated. After each stage, a short reflective period is required to clarify the problem and identify next steps, so that the process evolves logically.

An essential feature of action research is that it should be a democratic process in which new actions and attitudes are embedded in the school's practice, transforming its culture. Making changes to administrative processes, though sometimes necessary, will not be the whole story. For embedded change to succeed, it has to become a whole-school vision. Action research should be emancipatory in principle – that is, carried out *with* people and not done *to* them. As action research is collaborative, an initial step will be to find a group of committed colleagues who are prepared to challenge the status quo and also support change, who will act as the core change group. These might be representative of various parts of the school or of roles, depending on the chosen area to be developed. This group will help define goals for action and success criteria. Since action research is a collaborative process, conclusions should be shared with relevant colleagues. Evaluation within the action research cycle is how *validity* is tested. It will be colleagues who judge what works, so time should be set aside for meetings with this group and efficient feedback systems should be worked out. Remember that action research findings are not generalisable to other settings (for further reading on action research see *Source List*).

An understanding of change management helps effective planning for change and can, if used appropriately, mitigate many of the uncertainties for those experiencing change. Everyone and every organisation seeks stability because what is known is predictable and safe. Doing something different requires courage and a high level of trust between colleagues. Understanding the principles behind the change management process helps individuals and organisations to transition more effectively. The key, though, is to have a good sense of timing!

Knoster model (1991)

The strength of this change model is the identification of five aspects of change to be taken into account in order for successful change to take place. These are: vision, skills, incentives, resources and an action plan. The model suggests that if any of these elements are missing, then the change is likely to be difficult to achieve successfully (see *Appendix 10a*). The vision is the crucial starting point.

Developing and articulating what you want the organisation to be helps staff understand the end point. In managing change, asking what you want the change to look like well into the future and visualising how it will be from the point of view of all those involved in it will generate ideas, thoughts and phrases that can be distilled down to a short phrase or sentence that is memorable for all those involved. Expressing the vision as a result makes it dynamic and motivating. The vision underpins all the work that you do and drives the work to achieve the vision. When the vision is 'big' in everyone's mind, there are few barriers on the way. Where the vision is unclear or poorly articulated, many barriers may be erected and excuses made as to why change cannot happen. This can be measured by listening to the language used. 'I can if. . .' indicates there are few barriers, whereas 'yes, but. . .' demonstrates resistance.

Everyone involved in the change, including pupils, needs to understand the end result so they can, with help, plan their journey from current to new practice. Once the vision has been clearly articulated and agreed, shorter-term goals can be set and, from these, annual action plans drawn up. People at all levels are involved in change, and including everyone at an appropriate level reaps rewards. President Kennedy, on a tour of NASA, stopped to ask a cleaner what his job was; the response he received was 'to put a man on the moon, sir'! This is a man who shared the vision of the organisation.

Comparison of the Knoster model with the action research steps described earlier in the chapter shows some similarities. The first step of the Knoster model focuses on vision. This could be used to elaborate the problem illumination step, as could Fullan's ideas: Fullan (1999) describes the importance of organisations knowing what their core values and beliefs are. Such organisations are able to take on changes, especially from outside, that add to their sense of who they are and add value to what they are doing. Such organisations value learning for the whole community: pupils, teachers, support staff, parents and governors and anyone else who is part of the school community. In healthy organisations, Fullan argues, only those initiatives that will move them closer to their vision will be taken on board. Schools who refuse to take on any change because of an attitude that 'what we do has worked for the past 20 years, so why change it' will ossify and cease to function; schools at the other end of the spectrum, where the head takes on every single new initiative, will become chaotic. Staff do not have time to embed one new practice before another one is thrust upon them; there is no time to see if anything works and the sands are constantly shifting.

Work on the vision is usually preceded by analysis of what is working well. Self-evaluation identifies the strengths and weaknesses in current practice in any given area. Carrying out a SWOT analysis (strengths, weaknesses, opportunities and threats) helps to address the areas for development through your strengths. Taking account of the 'threats' – the things that might stop you from achieving your goal both inside and outside your school or setting – and the 'opportunities' – the people and practices that will support your change – helps to give a more rounded perspective on planning change and addresses your weaker areas. Carrying out a SWOT analysis with a range of interested and involved colleagues, parents and pupils, as appropriate, will give a well-rounded picture. A form of self-evaluation is usually carried out every year as part of a review and as a step toward planning the future.

Setting goals

Having articulated a vision and completed a self-evaluation exercise, the next step is to set goals for the interim steps needed to achieve the vision. Again, goals should be expressed as intended outcomes, explaining what will be seen once the goal is achieved. Goals will be the guide for creating action plans that enable the first steps to be taken along the change journey.

Action planning

Action planning involves the detail of what you are going to do in the immediate future to take you on your journey toward achieving your goals and vision. Departmental action plans will give direction to the whole team. The creation of individual action plans based on the department plan will pinpoint, for each team member, their path both individually and as part of the team. These do not need to be complex; in fact, simplicity is often best, because then only the most important priorities are stated. Action plans can take many forms, including mind mapping, tables and flow charts, and can be left to personal preference. Whatever the form taken, however, they should contain the same basic components. These include targets, what is to be done, who is involved, timescales, costs and resources needed, and, most importantly, success criteria that describe what the change will look like once completed. These steps will inform and perhaps modify what is to be done next. Targets should always be achievable and manageable. Again, the third action research step would be similar to this model, in that goals are set and success criteria decided. Evaluation and reflection are essential aspects of action research, and the Bolman and Deal model described next will help this reflective process throughout.

Bolman and Deal model (1997)

The Knoster model is very clear and is a linear model of change management. Bolman and Deal (1997) offer a complementary analysis of change management that takes into account the human aspects of change. They identify four frames that need to be taken into account in managing change. These are:

• Structural
• Human resources
• Political
• Symbolic

Structural refers to the structures in place that enable the organisation to run. These include the cycles of development planning, job descriptions, financial planning and monitoring and school policies and procedures. Without frameworks that standardise the way the school runs, work would be chaotic.

Taking account of the *human resources* frame means leaders recognise the importance of investment in a highly motivated and skilled workforce. Involving people in decision-making and supporting them by offering training and recognising their efforts and accomplishments results in colleagues feeling empowered, supported and confident. Enabling participation in change where decision-making is shared creates ownership of both the perceived 'problem' and the solution:

> Human resource assumptions emphasise the fit between individual and organisation. Where the fit is good, both benefit: individuals find satisfaction and meaning at work; the organisation makes effective use of individual talent and energy.
>
> (Bolman and Deal 1997: 140)

The *political* frame takes account of the differing views and opinions around change. Typically, SEN departments are less political than others in schools, but ignoring this aspect of change can be perilous! Harnessing dissent in a positive way, enabling those with concerns to voice them and allaying fears can turn cynics into very supportive colleagues. Creating arenas where these voices can be heard is essential. A simple way to achieve this is to ask all those who disagree to work together to voice their concerns. Similarly, those who support the change can produce the positives. By setting these opposing views side by side, it is possible to address the concerns through the positives and ensure that some of the unanticipated hurdles can be addressed before they become stumbling blocks.

The *symbolic* frame takes account of the history, both recent and past, that informs the change taking place. Acknowledging history values what has gone on before, including people's vested interests in past and current practice. Ignoring this can give a message of unimportance, where only the shiny new practice has worth. This can create a feeling of being undervalued, especially where previous successes are ignored. Carrying forward some of the 'old' into the 'new' provides continuity and acknowledges past efforts. For example: a special school in London was moving from a very decrepit building into new purpose-built premises. Everyone was excited and the new building was spacious, light and full of possibility. The headteacher arranged for a photographer to track their last few weeks in the old building, attending to every aspect of their work. Many photographs were mounted along the corridor walls in the new school, so that as children and staff moved around their new and exciting surroundings, they could acknowledge their lives in the previous building.

Story-telling is a symbolic way of making sense of change. Stories contain wisdom and humour, are entertaining and can be sources of influence. They are rooted in the past, move to the present and provide possibilities for the future. Stories have plots, characters and emotional and sensory detail (Cameron and Green 2009). Managers can use stories to describe exciting and awful aspects of the change and can engage staff using humour, fear, excitement and a range of other emotions. Stories help teams make sense of their own past, present and future and, if used well, can create a living story made by all of the players. As the change evolves, so does the story. The school mentioned earlier use their photographs as a story and regularly change the photos to keep the story and the journey current and relevant.

Stories are a useful tool to help change teams 'walk in someone else's shoes'. Our opinions, views and values are shaped by our past experiences and our personalities. Everyone has a unique view of the world which cannot be shared by others. Being able to see someone else's point of view in change management increases understanding. It is not necessary to agree, but it is important to see. This is not always an easy thing to do, but it is a skill that can be practised easily: simply asking two people to take turns to mirror a simple task such as making a cup of tea, or a walk in the park paying close attention to surroundings, demonstrates the different worlds we all inhabit. What your partner sees, hears and does may be very different to your experience. In managing change, providing opportunities for colleagues to understand the motivations and actions of others is important.

The four frames are four ways to:

• look at our own actions and the ways we function;
• understand life in organisations;
• examine the change process and how it unfolds;
• develop strategies for working toward change.

Bolman and Deal suggest four questions for change managers to address:

• Am I being clear about new roles and requirements?
• Am I paying attention to the needs and feelings of others?
• Am I providing a forum in which to hear opposition?
• Am I providing help to people so that they can let go of the familiar and move into a meaningful future?

When building change teams, Bolman and Deal argue that it is important to include people who work in each of the four frames, so that all aspects are addressed. Ignoring one frame can be perilous, and surrounding yourself with like-minded people may result in imbalance and a narrow view of how successful change can be achieved.

The ideas and practical advice offered in this chapter are the bedrock principles upon which to begin the process of leading and managing change. Keeping a balance between the structural side of change, where it is important to move from point A to point B, and the emotional and human aspects of change and how these can impact on individuals is the key to success. Setting realistic time scales and then adding in extra time reduces the chances of 'failure', because deadlines come and go. Change will often feel like juggling, and it is the ability to stand back and observe what is actually happening that will keep the change process on track. The cycle of action research is an important tool to aid tracking and helps maintain SENCos' control of the progress. The amount of support provided by the headteacher and SLT will also be important for change to become a reality.

CHAPTER 11

The SENCo's Role in Developing Inclusive Practice

This chapter has three purposes. First, it will debate some issues of the language of inclusion in relation to the standards agenda, using selected references from recent research or commentaries. Second, it will discuss some aspects of training by and for SENCos. Last, it will draw together themes from earlier chapters, showing how the SENCo's skills and knowledge might help them develop inclusive practice.

What is inclusive education?

Barton (1997: 233) stated that 'Inclusive education is about responding to diversity [. . .] it is about listening to unfamiliar voices, being open to empowering all members and celebrating differences in dignified ways'.

Florian (1998) amplifies this, saying that if inclusion is the opportunity for people with a disability to participate fully in all activities that typify everyday society, this transcends the concept of normalisation. This is an important idea, because it means changing attitudes so that those with disabilities are not treated as a minority group – labelled and given special treatment. It means *including* activities for everyone which previously might have been seen as activities 'only for a disabled group'.

The language of inclusion

Benjamin (2002), writing at a time when the government frequently used the term 'inclusion' in their standards guidance, challenged this language, and in particular the phrase 'valuing diversity', saying that 'such concepts lend a veneer of social justice to the standards agenda'. She defined this standards agenda as 'shorthand for a drive to improve students' performance in examinations', linked to 'regimes of surveillance and regulation, through . . . punitive inspection and information proliferation', commenting that 'the standards agenda demands a certain homogeneity in its construction of academically successful students' (Benjamin 2002: 323). Her case study of two very different girls on the autistic spectrum illustrates the way her school coped with the two agendas of inclusion and the standards agenda, which seems to assume that 'one curriculum can be made to fit everyone, and that, with the correct teaching, every student's 'needs' can be correctly assessed and measured. 'The daily reality', she notes, is that this 'is profoundly flawed, and that many students experience no success within it'.

Glazzard (2013) also talks about normative practices in schools, which make difference visible. He illustrates this with a case study reported by a teacher who worked in a resourced provision for children on the autistic spectrum. This teacher described 'the significant tensions for schools as they strive to become increasingly inclusive while also responding to the imperative of the standards agenda'. The school had focused on the social integration of those in the resourced unit, as this was seen as a priority for these pupils; however, when an Ofsted inspection of the school insisted that attainment for those on the autistic spectrum with severe difficulties be included with the mainstream school data, it damaged the school's overall record of performance. Glazzard concludes that 'while resourced provision offers a real opportunity for advancing inclusion, it can also promote insidious forms of exclusion' (2013: 95).

Rose (2014) reflects on the Glazzard (2013) studies and discusses the issues raised, pointing out their value as 'food for thought' and continuing that 'it would be wrong to suggest that the raising of standards and inclusion are incompatible'. He recognises the challenge of meeting the standards agenda and raising attainments of pupils who find difficulty in formal learning, due to the false focus on narrow academic outcomes. His recommendation is 'to ensure that our own elucidation of these terms is at the forefront of discussions to support a commitment that enables each pupil to learn, while recognising their individuality and their right to take their place in a more just society' (Rose 2014: 56).

Taking a wider view, Marshall (2008), writing as a retired HMI, reflects on school inspection for children with additional needs, including the establishment of Ofsted in 1992. He observes that standards and the curriculum have been a particular concern for successive governments – but, he asks, are standards something to aspire to but always out of reach? He notes that for children with learning difficulties, determining standards is extremely problematic and assessing whether satisfactory progress has been made is seldom straightforward. He questions whether 'the current arrangements for inspection [in mainstream schools], lacking as they do any immediate support or advice to schools, are making a significant contribution to the raising of standards . . . for the majority of children with additional needs' (Marshall 2008: 74).

Parental choice

It should be noted that the DfE Green Paper of 2011 removed any bias towards inclusion, although the National Curriculum for 2014 still has an inclusion statement. In 2012 Robertson noted that the Coalition government seemed to have consigned the term 'inclusion' to the recycle bin for the foreseeable future, in favour of a radically different system that transferred power to front-line professionals, parents and the local community. He commented that 'this political agenda to replace the value of inclusion with the value of parental choice or preference is challenging' (Robertson 2012: 79).

The SEND Code of Practice (DfE/DoH 2015), in paragraphs 9.78–9.80, emphasises parents' right to request a school when drafting the EHC plan. But do parents have a real choice? This is debated by Bajwa-Patel and Devecchi (2014), whose research found that for some parents there is 'nowhere that fits'. Parents want the school they choose to provide a safe environment, where social skills and confidence are a priority as well as academic advancement. They also put high value on knowledgeable staff. So, the researchers concluded, it was not necessarily a matter of parents wanting specialist provision, but rather that the quality of provision was what made the difference. Whatever choices parents may demand, the law requires that schools admit pupils with special educational needs as long as this is in keeping with the efficient use of resources and the efficient education of other children.

Stobbs (2014b) says because parents want someone who understands their child's needs, their assessment of the child's school is based on the expertise that is located there, adding that some parents give up the struggle to secure a mainstream place because of a lack of such staff expertise. This means that building expertise in mainstream schools is a priority for inclusion to work. Robertson (2012) firmly states that ongoing professional development opportunities should be regarded as an essential extension to the SENCo's role as teacher educator.

The SENCo's role in training and developing others

The SENCo's role in training and developing colleagues to meet the needs of children with SEN has been strengthened in the Code and can take different forms, from INSET days to role-modelling in classrooms. Training must respond to different purposes: to give staff the skills to meet general needs among the school population, for example training in listening skills; to enable staff to know how to meet the needs of a particular child or type of difficulty; and to meet demands for change resulting from government strategies and legislation.

Planning systematic training that is responsive to identified needs and monitoring its impacts is an important SENCo responsibility. It is tempting to over-plan training, so building time for reflective practice and discussion between colleagues is important in embedding new practices. Even when training has been systematic and shared with colleagues, the impact on pupil outcomes may not always be immediately apparent. Evaluations carried out at the end of a training session are useful to the trainer but planning for long-term impact means identifying the expected outcomes achievable within realistic time-scales and then monitoring whether they happen. Training should make an identifiable difference. To ensure appropriately targeted CPD is designed and implemented, it is useful to carry out an audit of staff needs and concerns or an impact analysis of the desired improved practice. This analysis looks at the *products, processes* and *outcomes* of the improved practice, and helps to plan activities and training to achieve the desired outcomes. (See *Activity 5*.)

Further training and development will depend on school priorities in relation to SEND, reflected in the school development plan. Working with senior leaders to plan training and development and set goals is important. Remember that SENCos do not have to do it all themselves – good practice among staff can be demonstrated in-house, training can be bought in, or it can take place outside the school. A planned sequence of regular short training sessions can have as much effect as an INSET day. However, training courses outside the school or setting will only add value if opportunities are provided to share the learning gained with relevant staff at school – and a single short session as part of a staff meeting is not enough.

Few teachers will have had significant training on SEN and disability in their initial teacher training (ITT). The Salt Review (DCSF 2010) identified how little ITT is available for those wanting to teach children with SLD and PMLD, 25 per cent of whom are in the mainstream. The Carter Review of Initial Teacher Training (DfE 2015) reported that ITT inadequately prepares new teachers to address SEND and recommended that the ITT framework should include training for SEND and practical strategies for effective differentiation. It also recommends research undertaken by teachers. The Code (2014) emphasises that as part of ensuring high quality teaching for all, schools should review and improve teachers' understanding of strategies to identify and support vulnerable pupils and their knowledge of the SEN most frequently encountered (DfE/DoH 2015: 6.37). Many special schools are working with the mainstream to exchange teachers and provide in-class opportunities to develop specialist skills in supporting children with high-level needs, including autism. There are a number of government and commercial online packages which offer specific and practical training to support high-quality teaching, which can be used by individuals or staff groups (see *Source List*). The NASEN library of resources provides a comprehensive list with websites. SENCos should make full use of such programmes and online publications, such as *SENCo Update*, for ongoing or sharply focused training for themselves and their colleagues.

Support and training for SENCos

SENCos themselves will require training to carry out their role effectively. New SENCos will undertake the mandatory NASENCO course described in *Chapter 1*, focusing on their dual roles of improving teaching and learning and leading and managing change. Various providers across the country offer different approaches, including face-to-face, online and blended learning: SENCos may choose their preferred style of learning and course duration. The opportunities afforded to undertake research, particularly action research, to make an impact on the workplace have been highly valued. Staff development through change management and action planning was explored in *Chapter 10*.

Research by Cowne (2005) on the impact of early SENCo training, based on TDA competencies, identified SENCos as agents of change, which is reinforced in the NASENCO training. The NASENCO training has had a significant positive impact on SENCos' personal professional development and in the whole-school approach to SEND policy and practice: collaborating with colleagues; making better use of data; raising expectations (Pearson and Gathercole 2011, cited in Griffiths and Dubsky 2012). This research found that positive outcomes of the NASENCO courses included increased awareness among SENCos of broader issues affecting their working lives and how to be a leader, not just a manager. SENCos can make better use of outside expertise. They report gains in confidence and feelings of increased status. The opportunities the courses afford for building networks and for mutual support are highly valued. Reading about research and policy and carrying out their own research has deepened SENCos' knowledge and understanding of theory underpinning practice. However, the negative impact of pressures on SENCos' time resulting from the extra work, including writing assignments, has proved difficult for many, especially those with families, as has been widely reported (Griffiths and Dubsky, 2012). School support for SENCos undertaking NASENCO will need to include additional study time and, ideally, a mentor in senior management to oversee and facilitate their studies in school. SENCos on training courses are often asked to develop an area of policy and practice for their coursework. By engaging in reflective conversations, the SENCo can act as an agent of change, opening up opportunities for change management. Cowne (2003) offers many practical examples of how SENCos on training courses have developed areas of school policy and practice.

SENCos developing inclusive practice

SENCos and teachers already know that inclusion is not a simple one-dimensional concept. At a strategic planning level, being an inclusive school requires a positive attitude from all who work in it, which affects the overall ethos of the school, its systems and organisation and the well-being of all within. Working towards more inclusive practice is thus a process which will be ongoing. If it is to be effective, teachers will have to work collaboratively and senior management will need to give their support. Inclusion depends on managing effective partnerships between teachers, support staff and parents, recognising each other's contributions. At another level, inclusion means that the curriculum on offer and the teaching that takes place in classrooms allow for diversity of learning styles, pace and focus. Such high-quality teaching allows pupils to participate fully in the learning process. At the third level, that of the individual child, inclusion is likely to be about friendship, self-esteem and relationships with the peer group and developing skills for independent life.

It may well be that part of a SENCo's role is to ensure that teachers and the peer group have training in disability issues, so that ignorance does not produce attitudes which make real inclusion impossible (DfE/DoH 2015: 6.37). As was discussed in *Chapter 6*, staff will require help in understanding how specific knowledge can reduce barriers to learning for pupils with disabilities. Often simple changes in classroom practices will help a broad range of pupils take a fuller part in the school curriculum and in school life. Each pupil is different and should have a say in how their learning is supported. The SENCo should always consider the individual needs of pupils who attend the school. One important way in which inclusive practice will move forward is if teachers listen to pupil and parent perspectives, and are prepared to adopt flexible practices which take on board individual differences.

One purpose of this final chapter is to examine the SENCo's role, in its totality, within the context of whole-school development. Schools are being challenged to become more effective by setting targets for improvement against national and indeed international standards. The SENCo will have an important part to play in a school's development by keeping the quality of teaching and learning for *all* pupils on the agenda. How does the child with special educational needs fare in this search for school improvement? Are they to be welcomed as part of a diverse community and valued for their contribution and achievements, or does the focus on ever-improving academic standards and publishing results make schools afraid to include these pupils on their roll? Inclusion does not end with placement. For a pupil to feel included, they should be able to take part socially and have friends. It will be very important for SENCos to listen to pupils' perspectives on their social well-being as well as monitoring academic progress.

One characteristic of a good school is that it has established good management of resources, which maximises the potential effectiveness of the whole institution. The resources of time, people and equipment will be required to meet the identified range of pupils with special needs. Policies will require strategic planning by those in management to include the careful monitoring of these resources, as discussed in *Chapter 5*. This policy and resource allocation must be clearly understood by everyone, including parents/carers.

However, a successful inclusion policy is as much to do with attitudes and values as resources. Developing effective inclusive education remains a challenge to most schools, even when it is a part of their mission. 'Society is made up of other people's children' was a remark frequently made by Joan Sallis (a guru of school governors from the 1980s to 90s) when talking to teachers. By this she meant that we cannot afford to educate only the high achievers or the easy-to-teach children, because every child will be part of our future.

Schools alone cannot achieve the change needed for an inclusive system. As Fullan (2003) proposes, change must happen on the three levels of government, local authority and school. Fullan explores what he calls this 'complexity theory' in depth and develops the idea of a learning community, where everyone is willing to learn together. Translating this into the inclusion debate means developing an ethos in which everyone's contribution is valued and respected, using the views of pupils, parents, TAs and teachers in everyday problem-solving and in longer-term policy-making. This could also mean building partnerships between schools, especially between special and mainstream schools. Some of the most successful inclusion projects have occurred where local authorities set an agenda and develop policies which support schools and their teachers, offering extensive and ongoing training for SENCos and specialist training for all staff. This all requires strong commitment and leadership.

Building constructs

Everyone builds up their own construct of special needs or inclusion from their experience and knowledge, both personal and professional. Research by Cowne (1993) demonstrated how, for course members, constructs developed as a result of attending courses and working on school-based practitioner research projects. SENCos and special needs teachers built up their confidence and competence by learning both the theory and practice of individual assessment and teaching, curriculum planning and differentiation, effective classroom management techniques and consultancy skills. Constructs grew in complexity as the teachers gained more experience and reflected on their own learning. Constructs were not fixed, although each individual had a core which was personal to them. It follows that the SENCo's role will also be built from an interaction between his or her constructs and those of significant numbers of the school's staff. Each school will build its value systems, out of which all the policies, priorities and roles will develop. It is only when SENCos are supported by heads, and by what one head called 'a critical number' of other staff, that change in the institution can occur. Headteachers' constructs of SEN are often different from their SENCos'. This may be because head teachers have other priorities. They often see SEN policy as helping to develop good classroom management and well-planned curriculum differentiation, resulting in better standards of teaching in their schools. SEN development therefore becomes a lever for other school improvements.

Using this book to help manage your role as a SENCo

Reviewing policy will include considering which tasks are to be performed by the SENCo along with other roles and responsibilities (*Chapter 2*), and the SENCo as a change agent (*Chapter 10*). Assessment and planning are important aspects of the role. There is a challenge when attempting to individualise support at the same time as diversifying resources to support a differentiated curriculum for all (*Chapters 3* and *4*). The inclusion of a wider range of pupils has resulted in more support personnel to manage and more multi-agency working (*Chapters 5* and *7*). Tensions exist between wishing to use time to support pupils, parents and colleagues (the consultative role; *Chapters 3, 4* and *6*) and dealing with paperwork and procedures (the co-ordinating role; *Chapters 8* and *9*).

This book has attempted to give practical advice, theoretical background and ideas to support SEN policy development and the SENCo's role within that development. Some readers will be experienced and for them, we hope to have stimulated thought and challenged them to take on further reading. Others will have been more recently appointed and will need the practical detail the book provides. However, this book does not have all the answers. Some questions require local knowledge; some further research. SENCos will need to keep themselves informed about new government initiatives and documents, while being able to challenge and critique the thinking behind such publications. SENCos will have a significant role to play as long as they remain reflective practitioners, able to manage change in themselves and hold meaningful conversations with colleagues, pupils and parents, to develop the expertise and attitudes to make ordinary schools special places for all pupils.

Whole-School Policy for Special Educational Needs

Activity 1 Audit of Whole-School Policy

Activity 2 Lesson Planning for Differentiation

Activity 3 Support Policy Review

Activity 4 SENCo Organisational Checklist

Activity 5 Impact and Analysis

Reviewing your Whole-School Policy for Special Educational Needs

The following exercise covers most aspects of a whole-school SEN policy. Select those that are most appropriate to your school. The aim is to give an opportunity for staff to discuss and reflect on what should be in the school's policy and how it is working at present. Areas for development and differing opinions may be revealed. These can be further explored in a discussion group.

If using this as a staff development exercise, individuals should work in small groups, such as year or curriculum teams, to reach some consensus of opinion on the most important priorities for the next year's work on the policy. This group activity starts by collating the group's individual results and looking for the biggest/smallest gap between the upper and lower line of markings.

Alternatively this audit could be given to staff as a questionnaire. Analysis of the data will provide information to the SENCo or the steering group.

Activity 1: Audit of Whole-School Policy

This checklist contains 17 statements about SEN policy or arrangements in schools. Its purpose is to help identify those points of your school's policy or practice where there is scope for improvement.

Each statement is followed by two lines – a) and b), for rating on a 1–5 scale.

Line a) – Ring the number which represents the extent to which you feel this **ought** to be in the whole school policy on SEN:

　　　1 = *must not be in*; 5 = *must be in.*

Line b) – Ring the number which represents your view of the **actual** situation at present:

　　　1 = *not happening at all*; 5 = *happening completely.*

If you wish, add two more statements to cover any aspects not already mentioned. Rank these in the same way as the others. The difference between the ratings of the two lines may indicate the school's most important areas for action. Discussion following this exercise within a staff or in-service meeting will serve as a way to reach consensus over priorities for the next year (concept developed from Evans *et al.* 1981).

1　There is an operational policy for SEN which has principles consistent with the Code of Practice (2015) (DfE/DoH 2015) and SEN Regulations (2014).
　　(a)　1　　　　2　　　　3　　　　4　　　　5
　　(b)　1　　　　2　　　　3　　　　4　　　　5

2　The key principles of the school's SEN policy are known to all staff.
　　(a)　1　　　　2　　　　3　　　　4　　　　5
　　(b)　1　　　　2　　　　3　　　　4　　　　5

3　There are descriptive guidelines on the roles and responsibilities of staff in relation to SEN. These include roles for governors, head, SENCos, teachers and TAs.
　　(a)　1　　　　2　　　　3　　　　4　　　　5
　　(b)　1　　　　2　　　　3　　　　4　　　　5

4　The progress of pupils with SEN is carefully monitored and evaluated, within whole-school assessment practice.
　　(a)　1　　　　2　　　　3　　　　4　　　　5
　　(b)　1　　　　2　　　　3　　　　4　　　　5

5　There are arrangements in place to organise regular reviews of progress for all pupils with SEN.
　　(a)　1　　　　2　　　　3　　　　4　　　　5
　　(b)　1　　　　2　　　　3　　　　4　　　　5

6　Pupils are involved in decision-making during the planning and review of their provision.
　　(a)　1　　　　2　　　　3　　　　4　　　　5
　　(b)　1　　　　2　　　　3　　　　4　　　　5

7 Staff are supported in the development of a range of teaching strategies, learning activities and support materials which enhance access to the curriculum for pupils with SEN.
   (a) 1   2   3   4   5
   (b) 1   2   3   4   5

8 Planning for pupils with SEN is an integral part of general curriculum planning.
   (a) 1   2   3   4   5
   (b) 1   2   3   4   5

9 There is a staff development policy for SEN which relates to the school improvement plan and reflects both school and individual priorities and needs.
   (a) 1   2   3   4   5
   (b) 1   2   3   4   5

10 Parents are involved in review and planning of provision for their child's additional needs.
   (a) 1   2   3   4   5
   (b) 1   2   3   4   5

11 Parents are given information about the school's policy and procedures for SEN, relevant to their child.
   (a) 1   2   3   4   5
   (b) 1   2   3   4   5

12 Support staff have clear roles and responsibilities and are encouraged to work as members of a team to enhance inclusive practice.
   (a) 1   2   3   4   5
   (b) 1   2   3   4   5

13 Liaison time is allocated for class or subject teachers to plan effectively with support staff.
   (a) 1   2   3   4   5
   (b) 1   2   3   4   5

14 The school's rationale for allocating resources for SEN is clearly described and made known to all staff.
   (a) 1   2   3   4   5
   (b) 1   2   3   4   5

15 There are clear procedures known to relevant staff for making referrals to outside agencies.
   (a) 1   2   3   4   5
   (b) 1   2   3   4   5

16 Disabled pupils and those with SEN have access to all aspects of school life including extended school activities.
   (a) 1   2   3   4   5
   (b) 1   2   3   4   5

17 The school's SEN Information Report is available on the school website and is regularly updated.
   (a) 1   2   3   4   5
   (b) 1   2   3   4   5

Activity 2: Lesson Planning for Differentiation

1 Choose a topic within your subject, suitable for one lesson.

2 Answer questions 1 and 2.

3 State core learning objectives and define learning outcomes for the lesson. What should the pupils learn? (Give range of outcomes if necessary.)

4 What resources will be required?

5 What different assessment modalities (such as oral, written, demonstration) will be used?

6 Write down prerequisite baseline skills or concepts that you are assuming are present in the class, before you start. (Change boxes to suit your needs.)

7 Once this has been done, think of children with specific needs and briefly define what difficulties, if any, they might have with your lesson as planned.

8 Write your modifications for these pupils. These might be prompts, support materials, ways of recording, etc.

9 If time allows, write extension ideas for able children.

Activity 2: Differentiation exercise for Key Stage 1 & 2 lessons

Question 1:
Is this realistic to do in the time allocated?

Question 2:
Is this relevant to this group of students?

Topic		Extension
Core curriculum objectives		
Strategies/methods/resources		
	How will outcomes be assessed?	
Modification		

Pre-requisite baseline skills

Language skills (written)	Social skills	Key concepts needed
Number skills	Organisational skills	
Language skills (oral)		
Manipulative		

Activity 2: Differentiation exercise for a Key Stage 3 lesson

Question 1:
Is this realistic to do in the time allocated?

Question 2:
Is this relevant to this group of students?

Topic		Extension
Core curriculum objectives – e.g. tasks, skills, concepts		
Delivery methods/resources/support		
How will outcomes be assessed?		

Modification		

Pre-requisite baseline skills

Linguistic	Social	Organisational	Subject specific
Numerical	Thinking	Other	

Activity 3: Support Policy Audit

Reviewing your whole-school policy and practice for managing support.

You are asked to mark the following statements on a scale of 1 to 5.

Line a) - According to your **ideal** view:

1 = *not necessary*; 5 = *highly necessary*

Line b) - According to how you view **actual** practice at the moment:

1 = *not happening at all*; 5 = *happening consistently*

Using the statements given below, mark your a) ideal and b) actual practice ratings.

Deployment

1   Teaching Assistants (TAs)/support staff have clearly written job descriptions which reflect their specific responsibilities, provided from the time they start their job in the school.
   (a) 1   2   3   4   5
   (b) 1   2   3   4   5

2   There is a clear structure for TA work in different roles and at different levels, including HLTA, across the school.
   (a) 1   2   3   4   5
   (b) 1   2   3   4   5

3   TAs' skills and expertise in particular areas of the curriculum are recognised and used in those subject areas.
   (a) 1   2   3   4   5
   (b) 1   2   3   4   5

4   TAs/support staff are line-managed by the SENCo or a member of SMT.
   (a) 1   2   3   4   5
   (b) 1   2   3   4   5

5   TAs have regular meetings as a team and/or with their line manager.
   (a) 1   2   3   4   5
   (b) 1   2   3   4   5

6   TAs are involved in performance management/review of their work.
   (a) 1   2   3   4   5
   (b) 1   2   3   4   5

7   TAs and teachers both work with the full range of abilities and needs.
   (a) 1   2   3   4   5
   (b) 1   2   3   4   5

Preparedness

8 TAs have useful induction training when they start working in the school.
   (a) 1   2   3   4   5
   (b) 1   2   3   4   5

9 TAs have a clear understanding of their role as part of a team, supporting teachers to support the pupils.
   (a) 1   2   3   4   5
   (b) 1   2   3   4   5

10 Teachers have a clear understanding of the TA role as part of the class team.
   (a) 1   2   3   4   5
   (b) 1   2   3   4   5

11 Teachers share and discuss their lesson plans with TAs.
   (a) 1   2   3   4   5
   (b) 1   2   3   4   5

12 TAs have regular meetings with their class/subject teachers to plan and review lessons and discuss pupil progress.
   (a) 1   2   3   4   5
   (b) 1   2   3   4   5

13 TAs are fully trained for the work that they do, including managing specialist interventions.
   (a) 1   2   3   4   5
   (b) 1   2   3   4   5

14 TAs have timetabled time for relevant preparation, meetings and record-keeping.
   (a) 1   2   3   4   5
   (b) 1   2   3   4   5

15 TAs share their skills and expertise in managing different types of SEND.
   (a) 1   2   3   4   5
   (b) 1   2   3   4   5

16 TAs participate in, and contribute to, ongoing professional development, as appropriate.
   (a) 1   2   3   4   5
   (b) 1   2   3   4   5

Practice

17 TAs encourage pupils to develop independence, to preserve their autonomy and to make appropriate choices.
   (a) 1   2   3   4   5
   (b) 1   2   3   4   5

18 TAs promote peer group acceptance and inclusion of all pupils.
   (a) 1   2   3   4   5
   (b) 1   2   3   4   5

19 TAs use supportive and positive language when working with pupils.
   (a) 1   2   3   4   5
   (b) 1   2   3   4   5

20 TAs use well-developed questioning skills to encourage pupils' learning.
   (a) 1   2   3   4   5
   (b) 1   2   3   4   5

21 TAs understand and use metacognition techniques and give useful feedback to pupils which assists
   their learning.
   (a) 1   2   3   4   5
   (b) 1   2   3   4   5

Whole-school issues

22 TAs/support staff follow safeguarding and child protection issues and procedures.
   (a) 1   2   3   4   5
   (b) 1   2   3   4   5

23 TAs are trained in effective behaviour management techniques.
   (a) 1   2   3   4   5
   (b) 1   2   3   4   5

If you wish, write your own additional sentence(s) to cover aspects of the policy and practice not covered
above. Rate these in the same way on an (a) and (b) line. You may also want to leave space for comments.

Activity 4: Organisational Checklist for Effective Management of Support

School: .... Date: ....

To manage provision for pupils with SEND effectively, SENCos must maintain an **overview** of school practice. However, carrying out these activities remains a whole-school responsibility. An organisational checklist may be helpful for SENCos to review the evidence of their progress in these areas:

Responsibility	Fully in place	Partly done	Needs development
Establish principles for TA deployment, with SLT and staff, and ensure that they are followed			
An operational collaborative working policy is in place			
Ensure that TAs have appropriate job descriptions that match the work they do			
Provide good induction and training programmes for TAs as a group and individually, matched to identified needs, including specialist programmes and teaching skills (e.g. questioning)			
Develop knowledge and skills in meeting SEND for all staff			
Develop teachers' skills in TA management			
Ensure that pupils, parents/carers and professionals working with the school have opportunities to give their views on support provided, and account is taken of these			
Ensure that teacher–TA liaison time takes place and that a record is kept and monitored of the planning, feedback and other discussions			
Check the planning for pupils with SEND at regular intervals and match this to teaching and to pupil progress			
Use lesson observations and other evidence to monitor the effectiveness of TA deployment within and outside classrooms			
Regularly and rigorously review the impact of classroom teaching and TA-led interventions on pupil progress			
Replace ineffective interventions with those that research has proved successful			
Hold regular meetings with TAs to ensure that shared issues are addressed and TAs are supported			
Ensure that TAs have regular reviews of their performance and constructive feedback			
Ensure that evidence of support and progress for pupils with SEND is available for parents/carers, governors, Ofsted and others			

Activity Pack

Activity 5: Impact and Analysis

Focus of Project: ....

Name of School: .... **Date:** ....

The purpose of this document is to ensure that training planned is closely matched to your needs and takes into account your previous experience and expertise. The analysis below helps plan sessions. This model incorporates expected impact into the initial stages of planning. An example would be the specific changes you might want to see in teachers' classroom strategies. Articulating our baseline practice and expected outcomes before designing the course helps to achieve this.

Products (these are the tangible outputs from development work, e.g. an improved policy, a new strategy document, establishment of network meetings etc.). **Baseline:** Our current practice is:	Impact: our improved practice will be:
Processes (these are the new or improved systems in schools, e.g. better planning processes, improved alignment between CPD and performance management). **Baseline:** Our current practice is:	Impact: our improved practice will be:
Outcomes (this is what you will see if the products and processes are effective. How do you know you are making or have made a difference?) Key questions are: • What have we achieved (as a result of the CPD activity) that is making a difference to the practice of staff, the school and children's learning? • What evidence is telling us that we are making a difference? **Impact** is the difference in staff behaviours, attitudes, skills and practice as a result of CPD **Baseline:** Our current practice is:	Impact: our improved practice will be:

Adapted from Earley and Porritt (eds.) (2009).

Appendices

129

Appendix 1a:
Categories of Disability
used by LEAs (1959)

These were listed as:

a) Blind pupils – pupils whose sight is so defective they require education by methods not using sight.
b) Partially sighted pupils – educated by special methods involving use of sight.
c) Deaf pupils.
d) Partially hearing pupils.
e) Educationally subnormal pupils.
f) Epileptic pupils – pupils who by reason of epilepsy cannot be educated under a normal regime.
g) Maladjusted pupils – emotional instability or disturbance.
h) Physically handicapped pupils.
i) Pupils suffering from speech defect.
j) Delicate pupils – pupils not falling under any other category who need a change of environment and who cannot without risk to health or educational development be educated under a normal regime of an ordinary school.

(Handicapped Pupils and Special Schools Regulation 1959)

The largest category of children requiring special education was those described as educationally subnormal (ESN). These were children who were said to be backward in basic subjects as well as those who were seen as 'dull'. Pupils with severe learning difficulties were not educated in schools at this time.

Appendix 1b:
Categories of Need
(2001)

The Code of Practice (2001) (DfES 2001a) introduced four areas of need, which largely remain the same in the SEND Code of Practice (DfE/DoH 2015). These four broad areas give an overview of the range of needs that should be planned for. The purpose of identification is to work out what action the school needs to take, not to fit a pupil into a category. In practice, individual children or young people often have needs that cut across all these areas, and their needs may change over time.

(DfE/DoH 2015: 6.27)

a) Cognition and Learning
        Specific Learning Difficulties (SpLD)
        Moderate Learning Difficulties (MLD)

Severe Learning Difficulties (SLD)
Profound and Multiple Learning Difficulties (PMLD)
b) Social, Emotional and Mental Health Difficulties
Changed from Behaviour, emotional and social difficulties (2001) to acknowledge the increasingly complex and common mental health difficulties many pupils experience and to recognise that behaviour can be a function of underlying difficulties.
c) Communication and Interaction
Speech, Language and Communication Needs (SLCN)
Autistic Spectrum Disorder (ASD)
d) Sensory and/or Physical Needs
Visual Impairment (VI)
Hearing Impairment (HI)
Multi-Sensory Impairment (MSI)
Physical Disability (PD)

Appendix 1c: Definition of Disability

The Equality Act (2010) states that a child or young person 'has a disability if he or she has a physical or mental impairment, which has a long-term and substantial adverse effect on his or her ability to carry out normal day-to-day activities'. This definition provides a relatively low threshold and includes more children than many people realise: 'long-term' is defined as a year or more and 'substantial' as more than minor or trivial'.

'Impairment' can be physical or mental. This includes sensory impairments, such as those affecting sight or hearing. Long-term health conditions are also included, such as asthma, diabetes, epilepsy and cancer. Children and young people with such conditions do not necessarily have SEN but there is a significant overlap between disabled children and young people and those with SEN. Where a disabled child or young person requires special educational provision, they will also be covered by the SEN definition.

The term 'mental impairment' is intended to cover a wide range of impairments relating to mental functioning, including what are often known as learning disabilities. (Equality Act, 2010, Chapter 15, Part 2, Chapter 1, Section 6).

Appendix 2a: Information that the governing body must publish in SEN Information Report

The Children and Families Act (2014), Part 3, SEND Regulations lists the SEN information which the governing body or proprietor of every maintained school, maintained nursery school and Academy school (other than a special school that is established in a hospital) must include in a report: this is set out in Schedule 1 Regulation 51 (as below).

1. The kinds of special educational needs for which provision is made at the school.
2. Information, in relation to mainstream schools and maintained nursery schools, about the school's policies for the identification and assessment of pupils with special educational needs.

3. Information about the school's policies for making provision for pupils with special educational needs whether or not pupils have EHC plans, including:

   a) how the school evaluates the effectiveness of its provision for such pupils;
   b) the school's arrangements for assessing and reviewing the progress of pupils with special educational needs;
   c) the school's approach to teaching pupils with special educational needs;
   d) how the school adapts the curriculum and learning environment for pupils with special educational needs;
   e) additional support for learning that is available to pupils with special educational needs;
   f) how the school enables pupils with SEN to engage in the activities of the school (including physical activities) together with children who do not have SEN;
   g) support that is available for improving the emotional, mental and social development of pupils with special educational needs.

4. In relation to mainstream schools and maintained nursery schools, the name and contact details of the SEN co-ordinator.
5. Information about the expertise and training of staff in relation to children and young people with special educational needs and about how specialist expertise will be secured.
6. Information about how equipment and facilities to support children and young people with special educational needs will be secured.
7. The arrangements for consulting parents of children with special educational needs about, and involving such parents in, the education of their child.
8. The arrangements for consulting young people with special educational needs about, and involving them in, their education.
9. Any arrangements made by the governing body or the proprietor relating to the treatment of complaints from parents of pupils with special educational needs concerning the provision made at the school.
10. How the governing body involves other bodies, including health and social services bodies, local authority support services and voluntary organisations, in meeting the needs of pupils with special educational needs and in supporting the families of such pupils.
11. The contact details of support services for parents of pupils with special educational needs, including those for arrangements made in accordance with clause 32.
12. The school's arrangements for supporting pupils with special educational needs in transferring between phases of education or in preparing for adulthood and independent living.
13. Information on where the local authority's local offer is published.

Appendix 2b: Governors' responsibilities with regard to SEND

Governing bodies and Academies have a duty under Part 3 of the Children and Families Act (2014), Special Education Needs and Disability Regulations (which replaces Part 4 of the Education Act 1996).

The governing body:

- is responsible for ensuring that the SEN and disability reforms are implemented in the school – the head teacher is responsible for the day-to-day delivery of the reforms;
- must ensure that the school has suitable arrangements for consulting with parents, informs parents when pupils receive support for special educational needs and involves them in reviews of progress;
- is responsible for ensuring that the school publishes information on its websites about the implementation of the governing body's policy for pupils with SEN (SEN Information Report, Section 69 Children and Families Act 2014): http://www.legislation.gov.uk/uksi/2014/1530/schedule/1/made;
- is responsible for ensuring that there is a qualified teacher designated as SENCo. A newly appointed person who has not previously been the SENCo at that or any other relevant school for a total period of more than 12 months must achieve a National Award in Special Educational Needs Co-ordination within three years of appointment;
- must ensure that the school is co-operating with the local authority, including in developing the local offer;
- must admit a young person when the school is named in an EHC plan in co-operation with the local authority;
- must ensure that arrangements are in place to support pupils with medical conditions (Section 100, Children and Families Act 2014);
- must ensure that the school meets the Equality Act duties for pupils with disabilities, including publishing information about arrangements for the admission of disabled children, the steps taken to prevent disabled children being treated less favourably than others, the facilities provided to assist disabled children' access and their accessibility plans;
- must have regard to the 0–25 SEND Code of Practice (DfE/DoH 2015);
- must use their best endeavours to meet pupils' SEN.

The responsible person is generally the head teacher, but may be the chair of the governing body or a governor appointed by the governing body to take that responsibility. If the responsible person is the head teacher, it is advisable to have one other governor with an interest in SEN.

Governing bodies and academy trusts are required, where reasonable, to provide auxiliary aids and services as part of the 'reasonable adjustments' duty. Technical guidance on schools' reasonable adjustment duties is available from the Equality and Human Rights Commission. These duties are set out in the Governors' Handbook, September 2014. The government has also produced a slide pack for school governors, available at www.nga.org.uk/Guidance/Pupils-and-parents/Pupil-wellbeing/DfE-information-on-SEND.aspx

Appendix 2c: SENCo responsibilities (SEND regulations 2014, 49–50)

The appropriate authority (e.g. governing body) of a school must determine the role of the SENCo and monitor the effectiveness of relationships between the leadership and management of the school, the SENCo's functions (as below) and the SENCo's effectiveness:

a) in relation to each of the registered pupils whom the SENCo considers may have special educational needs, informing a parent of the pupil that this may be the case as soon as is reasonably practicable;

b) in relation to each of the registered pupils who have special educational needs:

   i) identifying the pupil's special educational needs;
   ii) co-ordinating the making of special educational provision for the pupil which meets those needs;
   iii) monitoring the effectiveness of any special educational provision made for the pupil;
   iv) securing relevant services for the pupil where necessary;
   v) ensuring that records of the pupil's special educational needs and the special educational provision made to meet those needs are maintained and kept up to date;
   vi) liaising with and providing information to a parent of the pupil on a regular basis about that pupil's special educational needs and the special educational provision being made for those needs;
   vii) ensuring that, where the pupil transfers to another school or educational institution, all relevant information about the pupil's special educational needs and the special educational provision made to meet those needs is conveyed to the appropriate authority or (as the case may be) the proprietor of that school or institution;
   viii) promoting the pupil's inclusion in the school community and access to the school's curriculum, facilities and extra-curricular activities;

c) selecting, supervising and training learning support assistants who work with pupils with special educational needs;

d) advising teachers at the school about differentiated teaching methods appropriate for individual pupils with special educational needs;

e) contributing to in-service training for teachers at the school to assist them to carry out the tasks referred to in paragraph (b);

f) preparing and reviewing the information for the school's SEN information report.

Appendix 2d: Learning Outcomes for the National Award for SEN Co-ordination (NCTL 2014)

a) Professional knowledge and understanding:

- statutory and regulatory context for SEN and disability equality and the implications for practice in their school or work setting;
- principles and practice of leadership in different contexts;
- how SEN and disabilities affect pupils' participation and learning;
- strategies for improving outcomes for pupils with SEN and/or disabilities.

b) Leading and coordinating provision:

- work strategically with senior colleagues and governors;
- lead, develop and, where necessary, challenge senior leaders, colleagues and governors;
- critically evaluate evidence about learning, teaching and assessment in relation to pupils with SEN to inform practice and enable senior leaders and teachers;
- draw on external sources of support and expertise;
- develop, implement, monitor and evaluate systems.

c) Personal and professional qualities. The Award should enable SENCos to develop and demonstrate the personal and professional qualities and leadership they need to shape an ethos and culture based upon person-centred, inclusive practice in which the interests and needs of children and young people with SEN and/ or disabilities are at the heart of all that takes place. This is evident when:

- there are high expectations for all children and young people with SEN and/or disabilities;
- person-centred approaches build upon and extend the experiences, interests, skills and knowledge of children and young people with SEN and/or disabilities;
- the voice of children and young people with SEN and/or disabilities is heard and influences the decisions that are made about their learning and well-being;
- family leadership is encouraged and parents and carers are equal partners in securing their child's achievement, progress and well-being.

Appendix 2e:
Data chart

Beyond the macro-level data, SENCos could use a set of guiding questions to help them determine the other data they might need, and when these would be needed. Here are some questions a typical SENCo might be asking, and an indication of which data would be required to help with answering them:

What is our school SEN profile? What is the profile overall, by each year group, by each class?	• January census data. Live data on school's own database e.g. Integris. • Class lists
How does this profile compare to that of similar schools nationally?	• RAISEonline • SFR national data
Is this profile changing over time?	• School's own data • LA data • RAISEonline from previous years

What are we doing that is improving outcomes for our SEN pupils?	• Pupil progress data by Key Stage • Pupil progress data by area of SEN, e.g. MLD • Pupil progress data by Code of Practice, e.g. SEN without Statement/EHC plan and SEN with Statement/EHC plan • RAISEonline
	• Progress records linked to specific interventions • GEPs and IEPs, PCP and other plans • Annual reviews • SEN staffing and budget data/ provision map
What are we doing that is having little effect on outcomes for SEN pupils?	• Pupil progress data by Key Stage • Pupil progress data by area of SEN, e.g. MLD • Pupil progress data by Code of Practice, e.g. SEN without Statement/EHC plan and SEN with Statement/EHC plan • RAISEonline • Progress records linked to specific interventions • GEPs and IEPs, PCP and other plans • Annual reviews • Provision map
Are our SEN pupils making progress at least in line with other pupils in the school, given their ages and starting points?	• Pupil progress data by Key Stage • Pupil progress data by area of SEN, e.g. MLD • Pupil progress data by Code of Practice, e.g. SEN without Statement/EHC plan and SEN with Statement/EHC plan • RAISEonline • Group and individual progress records linked to specific interventions
What percentage of our SEN pupils are making good or outstanding progress?	• Individual pupil-level progress data
Over time, are outcomes for our pupils with SEN improving?	• Historic data such as previous years' RAISEonline

Are all SEN groups making good progress?	• Behaviour intervention records • Attendance records • Exclusions • Evidence of progress in other social and academic areas, including sports, music, drama • Qualitative data from staff, pupils and parents

Appendix 3: Children who speak English as an additional language and may have SEN

Bilingual learners are often classified by EAL teachers by their stages of development in learning English.

Bilingual Stages

Stage 1 – new to English
Stage 2 – learning familiarity with English
Stage 3 – becoming confident in use of English
Stage 4 – on the way to fluent use of English in most social learning contexts

• Find out how long the pupil has been learning English.
• Talk to parents about the child in the home context and what language(s) are spoken at home.
• Check health records and previous educational history.

It is important not to confuse difficulty with learning English and difficulty with learning per se. Pupils at an early stage of learning English should not be given SEN support unless SEND has been clearly identified. It takes up to two years to develop basic interpersonal communication. Pupils learning English as an additional language may be supported by teachers or TAs who speak their languages or who have expertise in supporting EAL, who can give advice on how to support and teach these pupils to acquire their new language while retaining the use of their own first language. NALDIC (the National Association for Language Development in the Curriculum) offers specialist advice: www.naldic.org.uk

The OFSTED guidance to inspectors on EAL (April 2013) refers to schools using 'A language in common: assessing English as an additional language' (QCA 2009). This is available at http://dera.ioe.ac.uk/4440/1/3359_language_in_common.pdf

Appendix 6a: Different ways of observing children

Observation is a way of finding out more, but first it is necessary to ask: Why observe? Answers could be:

• As a means of generating hypotheses.
• As a means of answering specific questions. How often does a child do that?

• As a way to better understand children and their viewpoints and behaviours.

This last point is the most relevant to those wishing to learn about pupil perspectives.

Next ask: What should we observe? This could be a matter of choosing the scale of the focus, either:

• large units of activity, e.g. playground behaviour, or
• specific activities, e.g. reading strategies, or
• facial expressions, gestures, eye movements within specific contexts.

Next ask: How should the observations be done? They could be in the form of:

• diaries; biographies over time, e.g. day, week;
• single-episode recording;
• time sampling, e.g. one minute every 15 minutes;
• event sampling: recording each specific type of event wherever it happens;
• tracking: observing the child in different contexts or with different adults over a fixed period.

What form will recording take?

• narrative descriptions;
• prepared checklists to tick or mark with symbols;
• audio or video-taped analysis.

All have advantages and some suit certain techniques best. Narrative is necessary for diaries, tracking and events sampling. Checklists are best for time sampling. A mixture of methods may produce the best all-round picture.

Consider the following cautions:

• all observations take time – analysis can be even more time-consuming;
• focus as much as possible; be selective but be aware of bias from this selection;
• note what you see, not your inferences – draw no conclusions without evidence;
• be aware of observer bias – two observers may produce a clearer picture of reality;
• try to see things from the pupil's perspective, not your own;
• prepare carefully to avoid missing things because you cannot record quickly or accurately enough;
• warn colleagues of your activities and do not underestimate pupils. They might ask what you are doing if your behaviour is too peculiar!
• What part will spoken language play? Will this be recorded with the observation and if so, how?
• How valid are your observations? Can you check these with the child?

Examples

Time sampling

Advantages

- useful when behaviours to be observed are frequent, or when behaviours are distinct and recognised early;
- takes less time if prepared well;
- provides quantifiable data;
- useful for baseline information.

Disadvantages

- does not tell us much about pupil perspectives;
- omits context and interaction between behaviours;
- can distort reality because cause and effect may not be noted.

Event sampling

Advantages

- useful to learn more about a selective type of behaviour in detail, or when a whole event can be recorded and analysed;
- where context, antecedents and consequences can be noted, is good for ABC analysis of behaviour;
- can be used for infrequent events;
- pupil views can be included.

Disadvantages

- more difficult to prepare for thoroughly;
- needs more analysis after the observation.

Tracking

Advantages

- useful for finding out the effects of different teachers and different experiences on a child to find out reasons for a behaviour.

Disadvantages

- taking the time to do this may be difficult;
- colleagues need to agree and understand purposes;
- being inconspicuous may be difficult. The observer may make pupil behaviours different;
- focus on one pupil might be difficult to disguise and could cause embarrassment. Observer's activity must be plausible to the peer group.

The best way may be to use a mixture of techniques and data and to balance one with another. *Remember* that observation material is confidential and must be used to provide information to solve a problem or gain useful information *to help the child or children*. Once used, it should not be kept in any way that could identify the pupil. Pupils and parents have rights over data in this regard.

Appendix 6b: Example of questionnaire for primary pupils

Use the faces to find out how children feel about your area of enquiry. Ask your questions orally and use the first two to get the group used to the idea of colouring in or ticking the face that is most like 'how they feel when. . .', for example, watching their favourite TV programme. Then ask 'how they feel when. . .' answering the research questions (this method was used in ILEA Research for eight-year-olds, looking into pupils' views about learning to read and write: ILEA Research and Statistics 1988).

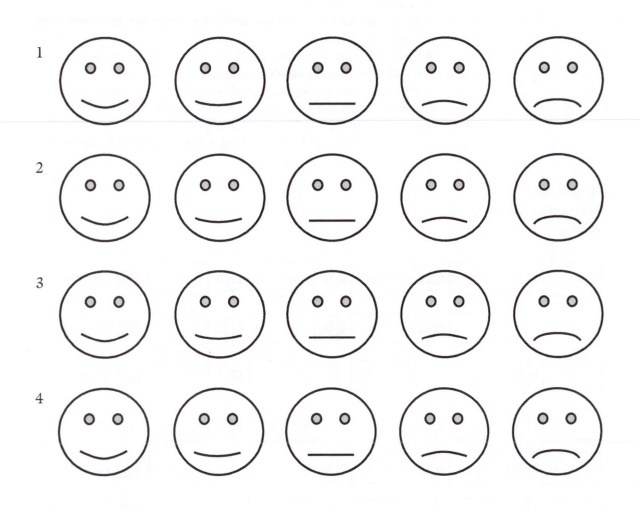

Appendix 6c: Definition of a parent (from glossary of code and the Children Act, 1989)

A parent includes any person who:

• is not a natural parent of the child, but who has parental responsibility for him or her, or
• has care of the child.

Parental responsibility under section 2 of the Children Act falls upon:

• all mothers and fathers who were married to each other at the time of the child's birth;
• mothers who were not married to the father at the time of the child's birth;

• fathers who were not married to the mother at the time of the child's birth, but who have parental responsibility either by agreement with the child's mother or through a court order.

Appendix 9: Advice and information for EHC assessments

• advice from the parent or young person;
• educational advice (usually from the school, but specialist teachers' advice may be added where applicable);
• medical advice (doctors and therapists);
• psychological advice;
• social care advice and information for or on behalf of the local authority;
• from Year 9 onwards, advice and information related to preparation for adulthood and independent living;
• advice and information requested by the child's parent or the young person (where the LA considers this reasonable);
• any other advice the LA considers appropriate.
      (From SEND Code of Practice DfE/DoH 2015: Chapter 9)

Appendix 10a: Managing complex change

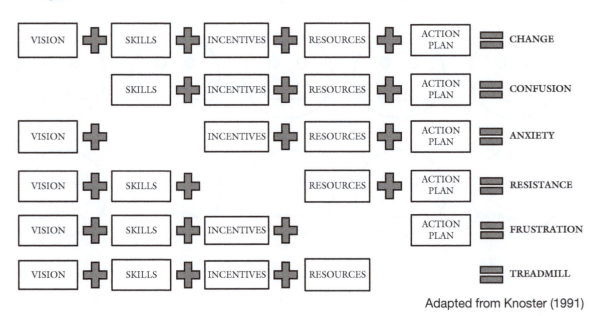

Adapted from Knoster (1991)

Appendix 10b: Action Plan example

Improving the Effectiveness of Teaching Assistants

Target	Strategies	Responsibility	Support/ Resources	Time scale	Success criteria/ Intended outcomes	Monitoring/ Review date
To improve the communication between the teacher and the TA; to improve impact of TA support of focused pupils	• Modify existing planning format to include a space dedicated for TA deployment. Within this space teachers will be required to plan whom they want the TA to work with, what the learning outcome of the lesson is for the focus group the TA is working with and have a note of any knowledge or resources the TA will need in order to be effective • Ensure time opportunities for teachers and TAs to clarify weekly planning	• SENCo – to be agreed by SLT then staff • Individual responsibility for action – teachers and TAs	• Support of HT and SLT in agreeing new planning format • Time for discussion/ clarification between teachers and TAs	• New planning format introduced as pilot Sept 2014 • Discussion and review of pilot and new planning format agreed by Nov 2014	• SC1 TAs to report feeling more prepared during lessons and not having to listen to the teacher to find out what the lesson was about • SC2 TAs to report feeling more confident that they know what to do during lessons, to support focus pupils • SC3 Evidence that TA support is now better focused, through pupil reports, responses and work	• Plans to be taken in and reviews by SENCO and SMT. Jan 2015 then termly • Interviews with teachers and TAs to discuss TA deployment, planning and preparation time • Pupil progress meetings to feed directly into evaluation of impact of TA support

Source List

Further Reading

Assessment

Black, P. and Wiliam, D. (2002) *Working Inside the Black Box: Assessment for Learning in the Classroom.* London: Kings College.

Clarke, S. (2014) *Outstanding Formative Assessment: Culture and Practice.* London: Hodder Education.

Davis, V., Buck, D. and Berger, A. (2001) *Assessing Pupils' Progress Using the P levels.* London: David Fulton Publishers.

Hall, D., Griffiths, D., Haslam, L. and Wilkin, Y. (2001) *Assessing the Needs of Bilingual Pupils: Living in Two Languages (Resource Materials for Teachers)(2nd edition)* Abingdon: David Fulton Publishers.

Hannell, G. (2014) *Identifying Special Needs: A Checklist for Individual Differences.* Abingdon: Routledge.

QCA (2009) *Planning, Teaching and Assessing the Curriculum for Pupils with Learning Difficulties.* London: QCA. www.teachfind.com/qcda/planning-teaching-and-assessing-curriculum-pupils-learning-difficulties-qcda-1.

Planning the curriculum

Byers, R. and Rose, R. (2004) *Planning the Curriculum for Pupils with SEN: A Practical Guide (2nd edition).* London: David Fulton Publishers.

Grove, N. (ed.) (2012) *Using Storytelling to Support Children and Adults with Special Needs. Transforming Lives through Telling Tales.* London: Routledge.

Hrekow, M. (2006) *Provision Management for Inclusion – Guidance Materials.* London: SENJIT.

Lewis, A. and Norwich, B. (eds) (2005) *Special Teaching for Special Children: Pedagogies for Inclusion.* Maidenhead: Open University Press.

Reason, R. and Boote, R. (1994) *Helping Children with Reading and Spelling: A Special Needs Manual.* London: Routledge.

Sassoon, R. (2003) *Handwriting: The Way to Teach It (2nd edition).* London: Paul Chapman Publishing.

Sassoon, R. (2007) *Handwriting Problems in Secondary Schools.* London: SAGE.

Tilstone, C., Lacey, P., Porter, J. and Robertson, C. (2000) *Pupils with Learning Difficulties in Mainstream Schools.* London: David Fulton Publishers.

Social, emotional and mental health difficulties and behaviour management

Barrow, G. and Newton, T. (2004) *Walking the Talk.* London: David Fulton Publishers.

Barrow, G., Bradshaw, E. and Newton, T. (2004) *Improving Behaviour and Raising Self-esteem in the Classroom.* London: David Fulton Publishers.

Boxall, B. and Benathan, M. (2013) *The Boxall Profile Handbook Revised.* London: The Nurture Group Network (for Primary).

Boxall, M., Benathan, M. and Calley, D. (2010) *The Boxall Profile for Young People.* London: The Nurture Group Network (for Secondary).

Ellis, S. and Tod, J. (2009) *Behaviour for Learning: Proactive Approaches to Behaviour Management.* Abingdon: Routledge.

Long, R. (2007) *Omnibus Edition of Better Behaviour.* London: Routledge.

Moseley, J. (n.d.) Jenny Mosley Consultancies. www.circle-time.co.uk

Riddock, B. (2012) *The Social and Emotional Assessment of Specific learning Difficulties.* London: Routledge.

Ripley, K. and Simpson, E. (2007) *First Steps to Emotional Literacy.* London: Fulton/Routledge.

Roffey, S. (2006) *Circle Time for Emotional Literacy.* London: Paul Chapman Publishing.

Rogers, B. (2000) *Classroom Behaviour – A Practical Guide to Effective Teaching, Behaviour Management and Colleague Support.* London: Books Education.

Person-centred planning

www.helensandersonassociates.co.uk

Disability information

Farrell, M. (2012) *Educating Special Children: An Introduction to provision for pupils with disabilities and disorders (2nd edition).* London: Routledge.

Hardy, C., Ogden, J., Newman, J. and Cooper, S. (2002) *Autism and ICT: A Guide for Teachers and Parents.* London: David Fulton Publishers.

Hull Learning Series (2004)*Hull Learning Series.* London: Routledge.

Inclusion Development Programmes (2008–9). Available at http://webarchive.nationalarchives.gov.uk/20100202100434/http:/national strategies.standards.dcsf.gov.uk/node/175591

Lee, M. G. (2004) *Co-ordination Difficulties: Practical Ways Forward.* London: David Fulton Publishers.

Lewis, A., Parsons, S. and Robertson, C. (2007) *My School, My Family, My Life: Telling It Like It Is.* University of Birmingham/ Disability Rights Commission.

Pickles, P. (2004) *Managing the Curriculum for Children with Severe Motor Difficulties.* London: David Fulton Publishers.

Powell, S. and Jordan, R. (2011) *Autism and Learning: A Guide to Good Practice.* London: Routledge.

Reid, G. (2012) *Dyslexia and Inclusion: Classroom Approaches for Assessment Teaching and Learning.* London: Routledge.

Riddick, B., Wolfe, J. and Lumsden, D. (2006) *Dyslexia: A Practical Guide for Teachers and Parents.* London: David Fulton Publishers.

Salisbury, R. (2008) (ed.) *Teaching Pupils with Visual Impairment: A Guide to Making the School Curriculum Accessible.* London: Routledge.

Research

Armstrong, F. and Moore, M. (eds) (2004) *Action Research in Inclusive Education; changing places, changing practices,changing minds:* London: Routledge/Falmer.

Greig, A., Taylor, J. and Mackay, T. (2012) *Doing Research with Children (3rd edition)*. London: Sage.

MacBeath, J. (1999) *Schools Must Speak for Themselves: The Case for School Self-Evaluation*. London: Routledge.

McNiff, J. (2013) *Action Research: Principles and Practice (3rd edition)*. Routledge: London.

NCSL (2005) *Getting Started with Networked Learning Walks*. Nottingham: National College for School Leadership.

Porter, J. and Lacey, P. (2005) *Researching Learning Difficulties: A Guide for Practitioners*. London: Paul Chapman.

Rose, R. and Grosvenor, I. (2001) *Doing Research in Special Education: Ideas into Practice*. London: Routledge.

Tilstone, C. (ed.) (1998) *Observing Teaching and Learning: Principles and Practice*. London: David Fulton Publishers.

Teaching assistants

Galloway, J. (2011) *ICT for Teaching Assistants (2nd edition)*. London: Fulton/Routledge.

O'Brien, T. and Garner, P. (eds) (2000) *Untold Stories: Learning Support Assistants and their Work*. Stoke on Trent: Trentham Books.

Russell, A. Webster, R. and Blatchford, P. (2013) *Maximising the Impact of Teaching Assistants: Guidance for School Leaders and Teachers*. Abingdon: Routledge.

Training materials

DfE (2012a) *Training Materials for Teachers of Learners with Severe, Profound and Complex Learning Difficulties*. Available at http://www.complexneeds.org.uk/

DfE (2012b) *Advanced Training Materials for Autism; Dyslexia; Speech, Language and Communication; Emotional, Social and Behavioural Difficulties; Moderate Learning Difficulties*. Available at http://www.advanced-training.org.uk/

Inclusion Development Programme. The Inclusion Development Programme is online government training for primary, secondary and EYFS teachers, on dyslexia, SLCN, autism and BESD, first outlined in Removing Barriers to Achievement (2008) and now available through NASEN. www.idponline.org.uk.

NCSL (2005) *Network Learning Communities Programme*. Available at http://networkedlearning.ncsl.org.uk/collections/network-research-series/summaries/nlg-what-makes-a-network-a-learning-network.pdf

Teacher Development Agency (TDA) (2006) *Teaching Assistant File*. London: Teacher Development Agency.

General

Gross, J. (2008) *Beating Bureaucracy in Special Educational Needs*. Abingdon: Routledge.

Hallett, F. and Hallett, G. (eds) (2010) *Transforming the Role of the SENCO: Achieving the National Award for SEN Coordination*. Maidenhead: Open University Press.

Tilstone, C. and Layton, L. (2004) *Child Development and teaching pupils with Special Educational Needs*. London: Routledge.

Wearmouth, J. (2011) *Special Educational Needs: The Basics.* London: Routledge.

Westwood, P. (2010) *Commonsense Methods for Children with Special Educational Needs.* London: Routledge.

Journals

British Journal of Special Education. NASEN Publications – www.nasen.org.uk

Journal of Research into Special Education. NASEN Publications – www.nasen.org.uk

SENCO Update (Monthly publication which informs SENCos of recent government documents and initiatives) – http://www.optimus-education.com/sign-senco-update-e-bulletin

Support for Learning. NASEN Publications – www.nasen.org.uk

Magazines

Special – NASEN Publications – www.nasen.org.uk

Voluntary Organisations

ACE Centre Advisory Trust

www.acecentre.org.uk
Free advice line: 0800 080 3115

ACE Education Advice & ACE Education Training

www.ace-ed.org.uk

Action on Hearing Loss (formerly Royal National Institute for the Deaf, RNID)

www.actiononhearingloss.org.uk
Freephone: 0808 808 0123
Textphone: 0808 808 9000
SMS: 0780 0000 360

Association for all Speech Impaired Children (AFASIC)

www.afasic.org.uk
Helpline: 0845 355 5577

British Dyslexia Association

www.bdadyslexia.org.uk
Helpline: 0333 405 4567 (Mon-Fri 10–12.30; 1–4pm; closed Wed pm).

Changing Faces

www.changingfaces.org.uk
Tel: 0845 4500 275 or 0207 391 9270
Support service helpline: 0300 012 0275

Contact-a-Family

www.cafamily.org.uk
Helpline: 0808 808 3555

Council for Disabled Children

www.councilfordisabledchildren.org.uk
Tel: 020 7843 1900
Council for Disabled Children, 8 Wakley Street, London, EC1V 7QE

CSIE – Centre for Studies on Inclusive Education

www.csie.org.uk
Tel: 0117 353 3150

Cystic Fibrosis Trust

www.cftrust.org.uk
Helpline: 0300 373 1000

Disability Alliance

www.disabilityrightsuk.org

Disabled Living Foundation

www.dlf.org.uk
Helpline: 0300 999 0004 (Mon–Fri 10–4)

Down's Syndrome Association (DSA)

www.downs-syndrome.org.uk
Helpline: 0333 1212 300

Epilepsy Action (British Epilepsy Association)

www.epilepsy.org.uk
Helpline: 0808 800 5050 (Mon–Thur 9–4.30; Fri 9–4)

Equality and Human Rights Commission

www.equalityhumanrights.com
Tel: 0808 800 0082

Independent Parental Special Education Advice (IPSEA)

www.ipsea.org.uk
Advice line: 0800 018 4016

ICAN

Advice to parents and practitioners about speech, language and communication

www.ican.org.uk
Tel: 0845 225 4071/020 7843 2510
Information: 0845 225 4073/020 7843 2552

KIDS

Advice on enabling disabled children, young people and their families

www.kids.org.uk

MENCAP

www.mencap.org.uk
Tel: 0808 808 1111 (Mon–Fri 9–5)

MIND

www.mind.org.uk
Mind*info*line: 0300 123 3393 (Mon–Fri 9–6)

National Association of Special Educational Needs (NASEN)

www.nasen.org.uk
Tel: 01827 311 500

Parents for Inclusion

www.parentsforinclusion.org
Admin: 020 7738 3888

Play Matters (formally National Association of Toy and Leisure Libraries)

www.ncb.org.uk/play-matters

Royal National Institute for the Blind (RNIB)

www.rnib.org.uk
Helpline: 0303 123 9999

SCOPE

www.scope.org.uk
Tel: 0808 800 3333 (Mon–Fri 9–5)

SENSE (Deaf/Blind Information and Advice Service)

Tel: 0300 330 9256/020 7520 0972
Textphone: 0300 330 9256/020 7520 0972
www.sense.org.uk

The Dyslexia Trust

www.thedyslexia-spldtrust.org.uk/

The National Autistic Society

www.nas.org.uk
Helpline: 0808 800 4104

The National Deaf Children's Society (NDCS)

www.ndcs.org.uk
Tel: 0808 800 8880 (Mon–Fri 9.30am–9.30pm; Fri 9.30–5)

The National Institute of Conductive Education

www.conductive-education.org.uk
Tel: 0121 442 5540

References

Note: apart from two important recent pieces of legislation, education acts of parliament have been omitted from this references list. Readers wishing to consult the texts of these various acts will find them at www.legislation.gov.uk/ukpga

Allan, J. (1999) *Actively Seeking Inclusion: Pupils with Special Needs in Mainstream Schools.* London: Falmer Press.

Audit Commission/HMI (1992) *Getting the Act Together – Provision for Pupils with Special Educational Needs: A Management Handbook for Schools and Local Education Authorities.* London: HMSO.

Bajwa-Patel, M. and Devecchi, C. (2014) 'Nowhere that fits' – the dilemmas of school choice for parents of children with statements of special educational needs (SEN) in England. *Support for Learning,* 29(2), 117–135.

Balshaw, M. (1999) *Help in the Classroom (2nd edition).* London: David Fulton Publishers.

Balshaw, M. and Farrell, P. (2002) *Teaching Assistants: Practical Strategies for Effective Classroom Support.* London: David Fulton.

Barton, L. (1997) Inclusive education: Romantic, subversive or realistic? *International Journal of Inclusive Education,* 1(3), 235–248.

Benjamin, S. (2002) Valuing diversity: A cliché for the 21st century? *International Journal of Inclusive Education,* 6(4), 309–324.

Bennett, C. (2014) Transition protocol. In NASEN (ed), *Everybody Included: The SEND Code of Practice Explained.* Tamworth: NASEN, 42–43. Available at www.nasen.org.uk.

Black, P. and Wiliam, D. (1998) *Inside the Black Box: Raising Standards through Classroom Assessment.* London: King's College.

Blagg, N., Ballinger, M. and Gardner, R. (1988) *Somerset Thinking Skills.* Taunton: Basil Blackwell and Somerset County Council.

Blatchford, P., Bassett, P., Brown, P., Koutsuobu, M., Martin, C., Russell, A. and Webster, R., with Rubie-Davies, C. (2008) *The Impact of Support Staff in Schools. Results from the Deployment and Impact of Support Staff Project (Strand 2 Wave 2).* [Research report DCSF-RR148 – The DISS Report]. London: DCSF.

Blatchford, P., Russell, A. and Webster, R. (2012a) *Reassessing the Impact of Teaching Assistants: How Research Challenges Practice and Policy.* Abingdon: Routledge.

Blatchford, P., Webster, R. and Russell, A. (2012b) *Challenging the Role and Deployment of Teaching Assistants in Mainstream Schools: The Impact on Schools – Final Report on the Effective Deployment of Teaching Assistants (EDTA) Project.* London: Institute of Education.

Bolman, L. and Deal, T. (1997) *Reframing Organisations: Artistry, Choice and Leadership (2nd edition)*. San Francisco, CA: Jossey-Bass.

Bruner, J. (1968) *Toward a Theory of Instruction*. New York, NY: W. W. Norton and Co.

Cameron, E. and Green, M. (2009) *Making Sense of Change Management: A Complete Guide to the Models, Tools and Techniques of Organizational Change (2nd edition)*. London: Kogan Page.

Carr, J. (2014) The EPIC effect. In NASEN (ed.), *Everybody Included: The SEND Code of Practice Explained*. Tamworth: NASEN, 24–25. Available at www.nasen.org.uk.

Carter, A. (2015) The Carter Review of Initial Teacher Training (ITT), DfE 00036-2015. Available at www.gov.uk/government/publications.

Children and Families Act 2014. Available at www.legislation.gov.uk/ukpga/2014/6/contents/enacted

Clarke, S. (2001) *Unlocking Formative Assessment – Practical Strategies for Enhancing Pupils' Learning in the Primary Classroom*. London: Hodder and Stoughton.

Cohen, L., Manion, L. and Morrison, K. (2000) *Research Methods in Education (5th edition)*. London: RoutledgeFalmer.

Covey, S. R. (1989) *The 7 Habits of Highly Effective People*. London: Simon and Schuster.

Cowne, E. A. (1993) *Conversational Uses of the Repertory Grid for Personal Learning and the Management of Change in Special Educational Needs*. Unpublished PhD thesis, Uxbridge: Brunel University.

Cowne, E. A. (2003) *Developing Inclusive Practice – the SENCO's Role in Managing Change*. London: David Fulton Publishers.

Cowne E. A. (2005) What do Special Educational Coordinators think they do? *Support for Learning*, 20(2), 61–67.

Dale, N. (1996) *Working with Families with Special Needs: Partnership and Practice*. London: Routledge.

DCSF (2008a) *Personalised Learning – a Practical Guide*. Nottingham: DCSF Publications. (DCSF/00844/2008)

DCSF (2008b) *Bercow Review of Services for Children and Young People (0–19) with Speech, Language and Communication Needs*. London: DCSF. (D16(7520)/0308)

DCSF (2008c) *The Assessment for Learning Strategy*. Nottingham: DCSF Publications. (DCSF/00341/2008)

DCSF (2008d) *Quality Standards for Special Educational Needs (SEN) Support and Outreach Services*. Nottingham: DCSF Publications. (DCSF/00582/2008)

DCSF (2009a) *Lamb Inquiry: Special Educational Needs and Parental Confidence*. Nottingham: DCSF Publications. (DCSF-01143-2009) Available at www.dcsf.gov.uk/lambinquiry

DCSF (2009b) *Progression Guidance 2009–10: Improving data to Raise Attainment and Maximise the Progress of Learners with Special Educational Needs, Learning Difficulties and Disabilities*. Nottingham: DCSF Publications. (00553-2009BKT-EN)

DCSF (2009c) *Achievement for All: The Structured Conversation: Handbook to Support Training*. London: DCSF. (01056-2009BKT-EN)

DCSF (2010) *Salt Review: Independent Review of Teacher Supply for Pupils with Severe, Profound and Multiple Learning Difficulties (SLD and PMLD)*. Nottingham: DCSF Publications. (DCSF-00195-2010)

DES (1978) *Special Educational Needs: Report of the Committee of Enquiry into the Education of Handicapped Children and Young People [The Warnock Report]*. London: HMSO. [Cmnd.7212]

DES (1983, 1984, 1985) *The In-service Training Grants Scheme, Circulars 1/83, 3/83, 4/84, 5/85.* London: HMSO.

DES (1983) *Circular 1/83: Assessments and Statements of Special Educational Needs.* London: HMSO.

DfE (1994) *The Code of Practice on the Identification and Assessment of Special Educational Needs.* London: Central Office of Information.

DfE (2001) *Handling Change Toolkit.* London: DfE.

DfE (2011) *Support and Aspiration: A New Approach to Special Educational Needs and Disability – A Consultation.* Norwich: The Stationery Office. (Cm 8027).

DfE (2012c) *School Funding Reform: Arrangements for 2013–14.* (DFE-00070-2012). Available at www.gov.uk/government/uploads/system/uploads/attachment_data/file/244364/school_funding_reform_-_final_2013-14_arrangements.pdf

DfE (2014a) *National Curriculum in England: Framework for Key Stages 1 to 4.* Available at www.gov.uk/government/publications/national-curriculum-in-england-framework-for-key-stages-1-to-4/the-national-curriculum-in-england-framework-for-key-stages-1-to-4

DfE (2014b) *Statutory Framework for the Early Years Foundation Stage.* London: DfE. (DFE-00337-2014). Available at www.gov.uk/government/uploads/system/uploads/attachment_data/file/335504/EYFS_framework_from_1_September_2014__with_clarification_note.pdf

DfE (2014c) *The Equality Act 2010 and Schools: Departmental Advice for School Leaders, School Staff, Governing Bodies and Local Authorities.* London: DfE. (DFE-00296-2013). Available at www.gov.uk/government/uploads/system/uploads/attachment_data/file/315587/Equality_Act_Advice_Final.pdf

DfE (2014d) *Keeping Children Safe in Education: Statutory Guidance for Schools and Colleges.* London: DfE. (DFE-00341-2014). Available at www.gov.uk/government/uploads/system/uploads/attachment_data/file/350747/Keeping_children_safe_in_education.pdf

DfE (2014e) *Statistical Release: Children with Special Educational Needs 2014: An analysis* (SFR/31/2014).

DfE/DoH (2015) *Special Educational Needs and Disability Code of Practice: 0–25 Years: Statutory Guidance for Organisations Who Work With and Support Children and Young People with Special Educational Needs and Disabilities.* London: DfE. (DFE-00205-2013). Available at www.gov.uk/government/uploads/system/uploads/attachment_data/file/398815/SEND_Code_of_Practice_January_2015.pdf

DfES (2001a) *Special Educational Needs Code of Practice.* Nottingham: DfES Publications. (London: DfES/0581/2001)

DfES (2001b) *Special Educational Needs Disability Act (SENDA).* London: The Stationery Office.

DfES (2003) *Excellence and Enjoyment: A Strategy for Primary Schools.* Available at http://webarchive.nationalarchives.gov.uk/20040722013944/http://dfes.gov.uk/primarydocument/pdfs/DfES-Primary-Ed.pdf

DfES (2004a) *Every Child Matters: Change for Children in Schools.* Nottingham: DfES Publications. (DfES/1081/2004)

DfES (2004b) *Removing Barriers to Achievement – The Government's Strategy for SEN.* Nottingham: DfES Publications. (DfES/0117/2004)

DRC (2002) *Disability Discrimination Act 1995 Part 4: Code of Practice for Schools.* London: The Stationery Office.

DRC (2005) *The Duty to Promote Disability Equality: Statutory Code of Practice.* London: The Stationery Office.

Donaldson, M. (1978) *Children's Minds.* Glasgow: Fontana.

Dweck, C. S. (2012) *Mindset: How You Can Fulfil Your Potential*. London: Constable and Robinson.

Earley, P. and Porritt, V. (eds) (2009) *Effective Practices in Continuing Professional Development: Lessons from Schools*. London: Institute of Education.

Education Endowment Foundation (2014) *Teaching and Learning Toolkit*. Available at http://educationendowmentfoundation.org.uk/toolkit/teaching-assistants/ (accessed 5.8.2014)

EHRC (2014) *Reasonable Adjustments for Disabled Pupils*. London: Equality and Human Rights Commission.

Equality Act 2010. Available at http://www.legislation.gov.uk/ukpga/2010/15/contents

Evans, J., Everard, B., Friend, J., Glazer, A., Norwich, B. and Welton, J. (1981) *Decision Making for Special Educational Needs – An Inter-service Resource Pack*. London: University of London, Institute of Education.

Feuerstein, R., Rand, Y., Hoffman, M. and Miller, R. (1980) *Instrumental Enrichment – An Intervention Program for Cognitive Modifiability*. Baltimore: University Press.

Fish, J. (1989) *What is Special Education?* Milton Keynes: Open University Press.

Florian, L. (1998) Inclusive practice. In Tilstone, C., Florian, L. and Rose, R. (eds) *Promoting Inclusive Practice*, pp. 1–7. London: Routledge.

Frankl, C. (2007) Using learning walks for sustainable CPD. *SENCO Update*, 90, November.

Frankl, C. (2008) Getting it all done! *NASEN Special*. September, 23–24.

Friswell, J. (2014) Assess – Plan – Do – Review. In NASEN (ed), *Everybody Included: The SEND Code of Practice Explained*. Tamworth: NASEN, 4–11. Available at www.nasen.org.uk

Fullan, M. (1999) *Change Forces: The Sequel*. London: RoutledgeFalmer.

Fullan, M. (2003) *Change Forces with a Vengeance*. London: RoutledgeFalmer.

Gardner, H. (1993) *Frames of Mind: The Theory of Multiple Intelligences*. New York: Basic Books.

Galloway, D. (1985) *Schools, Pupils and Special Educational Needs*. London: Croom Helm.

Gascoigne, E. (1995) *Working with Parents as Partners in SEN*. London: David Fulton Publishers.

Georgiades, N. and Phillimore, L. (1975) *The Myth of the Hero Innovator*. London: Birkbeck College, University of London.

Gerschel, L. (2005) The special educational needs coordinator's role in managing teaching assistants: The Greenwich experience. *Support for Learning*, 20(2), 69–76.

Gerschel, L. (2010) Unpublished teaching notes.

Gipps, C. (1992) *What We Know About Effective Primary Teaching*. London: Institute of Education and Tufnell Press.

Glazzard, J. (2013) Resourced provision: The impact of inclusive practices on a mainstream primary school. *Support for Learning*, 28(3), 92–96.

Goleman, D. (1996) *Emotional Intelligence: Why It Can Matter More Than IQ*. London: Bloomsbury Publishing.

Griffiths, D. and Dubsky, R. (2012) Evaluating the impact of the new National Award for SENCOs: Transforming landscapes or gardening in a gale? *British Journal of Sociology of Education*, 39(4), 164–172.

Hanko, G. (1995) *Special Needs in Ordinary Classrooms: From Staff Support to Staff Development (3rd edition)*. London: David Fulton Publishers.

Hargreaves, D., Beere, J., Swindells, M., Wise, D., Deforges, C., Goswami, U. and Wood, D. (2005) *About Learning: Report of the Learning Working Group*. London: DEMOS. Available at www.demos.co.uk/files/About_learning.pdf?1240939425

Hart, S. (1995) *Down a Different Path*. Discussion Paper 1, 33–42. In *Schools' SEN Policy Pack*. London: National Children's Bureau.

House of Commons Education and Skills Committee (2006) *Special Educational Needs,* Vol. 1. Ref: HC478-1. London: The Stationery Office.

Inhelder, B. and Piaget, J. (1958) *The Growth of Logical Thinking*. London: Routledge and Kegan Paul.

Kemmis, S. and McTaggart, R. (eds) (1992) *The Action Research Planner (3rd edition)*. Victoria, Australia: Deakin University Press.

Knoster, T. (1991) Factors in managing complex change. Presentation at *The Association for Severe Handicap Conference*, June, Washington DC, USA.

Layton, L. (2005) Special educational needs coordinators and leadership: A role too far? *Support for Learning*, 20(2), 53–60.

MacConville, R., Dedridge, S., Gyulai, A., Palmer, J. and Rhys-Davies, L. (2007) *Looking at Inclusion: Listening to the Voices of Young People*. London: Paul Chapman.

MacGilchrist, B. and Buttress, M. (2005) *Transforming Learning and Teaching*. London: Paul Chapman.

Mackenzie, S. (2007) A review of recent developments in the role of the SENCo in the UK. *British Journal of Sociology of Education*, 34(4), 212–218.

Mansell, W. (2014) Are welfare cuts hurting pupils who need help? *Education Guardian*, 27 May, p. 30.

Marshall, C. (2008) 35 years of school inspection: Raising educational standards for children with additional needs? *British Journal of Sociology of Education*, 35(2), 69–77.

MoE (1959) *The Handicapped Pupils and Special Schools Regulations*. London: HMSO.

Montgomery, D. (2003) *Gifted and Talented Children with Special Educational Needs: Double Exceptionality*. London: NACE/Fulton.

Murray, J. (2014) We've got a kid who hears voices: God knows when he'll get help. *Education Guardian*, 29 July, p. 28.

NUT (2004) *Special Educational Needs Coordinators and the Revised Code of Practice: An NUT Survey*. London: National Union of Teachers.

O'Brien, T. and Guiney, D. (2001) *Differentiation in Teaching and Learning: Principles and Practice*. London: Continuum.

Office of Qualifications and Examinations Regulation (OFQUAL) (2013) *Qualifications and Credit Framework*. Available at http://ofqual.gov.uk/qualifications-and-assessments/qualification-frameworks/

Ofsted (1996) *Promoting High Achievement for Pupils with SEN*. London: HMSO.

Ofsted (2006) *Inclusion: Does It Matter Where Pupils Are Taught?* London: HMSO.

Ofsted (2010) *The Special Educational Needs and Disability Review: A Statement is not Enough*. Manchester: Ofsted.

Ofsted (2014) *The School Inspection Handbook*. Manchester: Ofsted.

Oldham, J. and Radford, J. (2011) Secondary SENCO leadership: A universal or a specialist role? *British Journal of Sociology of Education*, 38(3), 126–134.

Robertson, R. (2012) Special educational needs and disability co-ordination in a changing policy landscape: making sense of policy from a SENCo's perspective. *Support for Learning*, 27(2), 77–83.

Robertson, C. (2013) Expert overview of the Local Offer. *Optimus Education*, October. Available at www.optimus-education.com/expert-overview-local-offer

Roffey, S. and Parry, J. (2013) *Special Needs in the Early Years: Supporting Collaboration, Communication and Co-Ordination (3rd edition)*. Abingdon: Routledge.

Rosen-Webb, S. M. (2011) Nobody tells you how to be a SENCO. *British Journal of Sociology of Education*, 38(4), 159–168.

Rose, R. (2014) Inclusion and the standards agenda: A reflective commentary. *Support for Learning*, 29(1), 54–56.

Russell, A., Webster, R. and Blatchford, P. (2013) *Maximising the Impact of Teaching Assistants: Guidance for School Leaders and Teachers*. Abingdon: Routledge.

Sebba, J., Brown, N., Steward, S., Galton, M. and James, M., with Celento, N. and Boddy, P. (2007) *An Investigation of Personalised Learning: Approaches Used by Schools*. London: DfES.

Skinner, B. F. (1974) *About Behaviourism*. London: Jonathan Cape.

Special Educational Needs and Disability Regulations 2014 (SI 2014/1530). Available at www.legislation.gov.uk/uksi/2014/1530/contents/made

Stobbs, P. (2014a) Participating in decision making. In NASEN (ed.), *Everybody Included: The SEND Code of Practice Explained*. Tamworth: NASEN, 39–41. Available at www.nasen.org.uk

Stobbs, P. (2014b) Overview of previous national SEND achievements and their fit with current SEN policy directions. *Journal of Research in Special Educational Needs*, 14(2), 128–132.

Szwed, C. (2007) Reconsidering the role of the primary special educational needs co-ordinator: Policy, practice and future priorities. *British Journal of Special Education*, 34(2), 96–104.

Teacher Training Agency (1998) *National Standards for Special Educational Needs Co-ordinators*. London: TTA.

Tissot, C. (2013) The role of SENCos as leaders. *British Journal of Sociology of Education*, 40(1), 33–40.

Tomlinson, S. (1982) *A Sociology of Special Education*. London: Routledge and Kegan Paul.

Training and Development Agency for Schools (TDAS) (2010) *National Occupational Standards for Supporting Teaching Learning*. Manchester: Training and Development Agency for Schools.

Tutt, R. (2007) *Every Child Included*. London: Paul Chapman.

United Nations (1989) *Convention on the Rights of the Child*. London: Unicef UK. Available at www.unicef.org/crc/index_30160.html

Vygotsky, L. S. (1978) *Mind in Society*. Cambridge, MA: Harvard University Press.

Watkins, C., Carnell, E., Wagner, P. and Whalley, C. (2001) Learning about learning enhances performance. *Institute of Education NSIN*, Research Matters Series 13.

Webster, R. and Blatchford, P. (2013) Re-thinking the TA role. *Special*, May, 12–14.

Wedell, K. (1978) Early identification and compensatory interaction. In Knights, R. M. and Bakker, D. J. (eds) *Treatment of Hyperactive and Learning Disordered Children*, pp. 13–22. Baltimore: University Park Press.

Wedell, K. (2005) The Gulliford Lecture – Dilemmas in the quest for inclusion. *British Journal of Sociology of Education*, 32(1), 3–11.

Wedell, K. (2006) Points from the SENCo-Forum: The spectre of homework. *British Journal of Sociology of Education*, 33(2), 98.

Wedell, K. (2014) Points from the SENCo Forum: A dilemma in 'personalised' teaching. *British Journal of Sociology of Education*, 41(1), 105–106.

Weller, K. and Craft, A. (1983) *Making Up Our Minds: An Exploratory Study of Instrumental Enrichment.* London: Schools Council.

Wragg, E. C. (1997) *The Cubic Curriculum.* London: Routledge.

Index

Page numbers in **bold** refer to main entries